ENTREPRENEURSHIP FOR DEPRIVED COMMUNITIES

ENTREPRENEURSHIP FOR DEPRIVED COMMUNITIES

Developing Opportunities, Capabilities and Enterprise Culture

BY

NIKOLAI MOURAVIEV
Abertay University, United Kingdom

AND

ALEX AVRAMENKO
Abertay University, United Kingdom

emerald
PUBLISHING

United Kingdom – North America – Japan – India
Malaysia – China

Emerald Publishing Limited
Howard House, Wagon Lane, Bingley BD16 1WA, UK

First edition 2020

British Library Cataloguing in Publication Data
A catalogue record for this book is available from the British Library

ISBN: 978-1-78973-988-6 (Print)
ISBN: 978-1-78973-985-5 (Online)
ISBN: 978-1-78973-987-9 (Epub)

INVESTOR IN PEOPLE

CONTENTS

LIST OF FIGURES

LIST OF TABLES

ABOUT THE AUTHORS

Dr Nikolai Mouraviev is a Senior Lecturer in Business and Management at Abertay University, Dundee, Scotland, UK. Previously he has held teaching positions at KIMEP University, Kazakhstan; Wayne State University, US; and Viterbo University, US. Part of his research focuses on public–private collaboration in developing nations and he has published extensively in this area. In addition, his research interests include entrepreneurship, particularly in cosmopolitan cities, and governance of the energy sector. Dr Mouraviev has co-authored five books, including one research monograph, and published more than 50 papers.

Dr Alex Avramenko is an experienced entrepreneur who returned to academia and completed his MBA and PhD in Management, to share his entrepreneurial experience and to advance research in entrepreneurship, particularly in rural contexts. For the last 10+ years, Alex has been lecturing for the Salford Business School and the Dundee Business School in Europe (UK, Austria and Latvia) and Southeast Asia (Malaysia). His research interests include digital, rural and energy entrepreneurship, as well as innovations in teaching and learning practice in Higher Education. Alex has published extensively and shared his knowledge within the domain of management consultancy.

ACKNOWLEDGEMENT

The significant part of Chapter 5 has been previously published as:

Mouraviev, N. and Kakabadse, N. 2016. Conceptualising cosmopolitanism and entrepreneurship through the lens of the three-dimensional theory of power. *Society and Business Review*, 11(3), 242–256.

1

INTRODUCTION: TOWARDS A MODEL FOR DEVELOPING AN ENTERPRISE CULTURE IN DEPRIVED COMMUNITIES

Revitalising deprived areas, and improving the living conditions of communities in such areas, has been and remains a challenging task for governments, NGOs and their private sector partners. Local authorities recognise that developing an entrepreneurial culture is key to creating 'enterprise readiness': this entails promoting a holistic understanding of business opportunities, raising the aspirations and confidence of potential entrepreneurs, and engaging disadvantaged neighbourhoods by means of life planning and initial support of their ventures (Dubina and Carayannis, 2016). Although the development of enterprise is viewed as a core element in the renewal of deprived areas, the shaping and delivery of viable and sustainable action appears to remain difficult for most local authorities (Estrin et al., 2013).

Throughout this book, the term *deprived community* is used. However, this is entirely for want of a better term as there is currently no single agreed definition of a deprived community. There are, in fact, many kinds of deprived communities. 'Deprived community' may refer to a poorer area with a low-income population, often characterised by persistent poverty, lack of employment opportunities and possibly a high crime rate. Another way in which the term 'deprived community' is used is in reference to a particular group that might equally be termed a 'disadvantaged population'. For example, single mothers or senior citizens may appear disadvantaged with regard to lack of support for their entrepreneurial initiatives, lack of knowledge and skills or, importantly, lack of entrepreneurial culture. In this book the term *deprived* will be used to describe either impoverished areas, or, depending on the context, people belonging to these communities, i.e. those who are disadvantaged, in need and/or in reduced circumstances. Such people do not necessarily reside in a deprived area; rather, they are grouped because they share same or similar needs. To summarise, this book will not only examine deprived communities in the sense of poorer areas that require revitalisation, but it will also adopt the view that a group experiencing similar disadvantages also constitutes a community, and not necessarily a geographical one. Of course, not all needs can be addressed by means of entrepreneurship, but this book will show that this approach has proven effective in solving a broad range of community challenges (Growing Inclusive Markets Initiative, 2008).

Within a broad theme of entrepreneurship, this book focuses on developing enterprise in and for deprived communities, which is a task of critical importance for the local authorities as these communities often display persistent poverty and other related problems (poor living conditions, deterioration of public services and high crime rate). Given the context of these urban and rural areas, the book offers the tools for revitalising the depressed neighbourhoods. Furthermore, it proposes a holistic model that integrates a range of dimensions in an innovative pathway for enterprise development in deprived communities. For example, the book shows that government support, training and empowerment of senior citizens are instrumental for developing of their entrepreneurship and, therefore, avoid deprivation of a certain group who otherwise might be viewed as low-income (London et al., 2010). In relation to lifestyle entrepreneurship, the book emphasises a need to promote *lifelong* approach to resource development in deprived communities, which is an essential part of entrepreneurial culture (McMullen and Dimov, 2013; Hanson et al., 2019).

The book aims to investigate the best practice of developing enterprise in and for deprived communities. It highlights a toolset of ideas that could be used by the local authorities to revitalise these areas and encourage disadvantaged lay people to launch small businesses (Oughton and Wheelock, 2003). Part of the book draws on the authors' own work in pilot projects commissioned by Manchester and Salford City Councils in the United Kingdom to support people that are currently out of the labour market to help them consider entrepreneurial ventures and self-employment as an option. Other chapters make use of the authors' research on the social entrepreneurship theme in Ukraine and on how urban governance advances entrepreneurial culture in cosmopolitan Dubai. The book also offers research-based narratives about rural entrepreneurship, engagement of senior citizens in launching micro and small enterprises, and about conditions for supporting enterprising activities in cosmopolitan cities.

The book's key themes are:

- New dimensions and opportunities of micro enterprise;
- Rural entrepreneurship;
- Engagement of senior citizens in enterprise;

- Lifestyle entrepreneurship;
- Entrepreneurship in cosmopolitan cities;
- Impact of social entrepreneurship on community development and furthering entrepreneurial culture; and
- Insights into a model for developing enterprise culture by highlighting facilitating and hindering factors related to deprived communities.

As this list shows, the book captures a broad range of topics related to entrepreneurship in deprived communities. This is because there are numerous tools that could be useful to many kinds of areas and neighbourhoods. For example, Chapter 6 discusses social entrepreneurship as a tool that focuses on supporting disadvantaged citizens (war veterans, low-skilled, disabled people), rather than a deprived community located in a certain geographical area. The book's purpose here is to emphasise that support of disadvantaged would alleviate poverty of certain groups, and this tool could be used in many communities. Ukraine is used as an example, which shows that social entrepreneurship could be encouraged and successfully furthered not only in an industrialised nation, such as Germany, the United Kingdom or the United States, but also in a developing country. In addition, Chapter 6 also demonstrates how social entrepreneurship could effectively serve – using non-traditional tools – the needs of a community, such as an urban area.

The book's unifying overall thread is development of entrepreneurial culture, and the book offers many tools that communities, their leaders and citizens might utilise to develop this culture. The book views entrepreneurial culture as behaviour, habits, attitudes and values that make continuous use of a set of qualities and conditions that are required to succeed as an entrepreneur (Fletcher et al., 2012). As entrepreneurial culture effectively serves as the book's theoretical framework, it explains why certain topics were selected for this monograph and how they fit the overall theme.

What makes this book special? The book offers an exclusive focus on deprived communities and how entrepreneurship could be developed there. Books that have enterprise in disadvantaged areas as their sole theme are hard to find. This monograph draws on real-life global experiences of community revitalisation projects and blends analysis of project implementation with conceptual approach to policy and governance in urban and rural areas. This shows enterprise development in action and departs from merely theoretical considerations. Furthermore, the book offers a model for developing an inclusive enterprise culture in deprived communities in the form of identified hindering and facilitating factors. As the model integrates a range of dimensions in a collaborative pathway for enterprise development, the book offers a set of innovative practical tools that enable opportunity creation and recognition in deprived communities and expedite capacity and skill building among disadvantaged groups. Each chapter provides learning points at the end (except the Introduction and Conclusion) which draw the reader's attention to facilitating factors and effective tools that may promote entrepreneurship in deprived communities. These learning points might be particularly appealing to those readers who are looking for a succinct summary of instruments and methods for the development of entrepreneurship.

For whom is this book? Academics, students and practitioners may equally benefit from the blend of chapters that reinforce the book's main argument that entrepreneurial culture is key to revitalisation of deprived areas and supporting disadvantaged populations. To this end, this monograph identifies a range of tools that local governing bodies, businesses, NGOs and social activists could use to form and/or contribute to entrepreneurial culture and engage disadvantaged groups in productive economic activity. This is likely to be of interest to a broad readership including politicians, local government staff, development workers, NGO activists and business people who are interested in revitalising depressed urban and rural neighbourhoods.

Practitioners may find the book useful as it highlights an array of real-life situations and problems that communities encounter, be it a case of an impoverished area with little to no jobs and discouraged job seekers or a community group who might be disadvantaged owing to their disability, family status or lack of knowledge and skills. The discussion of tools available for fostering entrepreneurial culture, followed by critical appraisal, will be of interest to readers in many communities across the globe as different contexts may require different approaches, instruments and methods (Welter, 2011). Practitioners may identify differences and commonalities in how local governments, activists and other stakeholders develop entrepreneurial culture and compare to the conditions in their own communities, which might be helpful for studying best practice or borrowing from the experience of other areas and/or projects supporting disadvantaged populations. By reading this book, practitioners may identify conceptual frameworks for working with deprived communities, and use these frameworks to shape the action plans engaging the local governing bodies, businesses and activists.

Researchers and students may also benefit from reading this monograph, as the book offers a unique blend of conceptual approaches and practical advice in a field that draws attention of many theorists. Readers will have an opportunity to compare a broad range of issues related to deprived communities and assess, from their own perspective, the effectiveness of the tools that the book offers and whether they are conceptually sound. For lecturers and their students, the book's suggestions might become the subject of debates in a classroom, which might facilitate their learning experience in the fields of development, entrepreneurship, regional and urban studies, policy, governance and strategic planning.

In summary, the book offers an evaluation of the enterprising projects in many nations and contexts and highlights a range of issues and tools related to developing enterprise in deprived communities. It shows how local authorities, in partnership with other actors, may implement an integrative approach to supporting disadvantaged groups by capacity and skill building. In addition to the array of tools helping to revitalise the needy communities, the book provides insights into developing an enterprise culture, which could serve as an effective and innovative instrument for improving conditions in deprived neighbourhoods. The key message is that commissioners of enterprise support need to employ collaborative approach to ensure that an integrated pathway is in place to help people sailing through the enterprise journey and to foster entrepreneurship in a community. Owing to the blend of theory, practice and related critical appraisal, this book may attract a wide spectrum of readers who are passionate about community activism and interested in poverty alleviation, local development and entrepreneurship.

REFERENCES

Dubina, I.N. and Carayannis, E.G. Eds 2016. *Creativity, Innovation, and Entrepreneurship Across Cultures: Theory and Practices*, New York, NY, Springer.

Estrin, S., Mickiewicz, T. and Stephan, U. 2013. Entrepreneurship, social capital, and institutions: social and commercial entrepreneurship across nations, *Entrepreneurship: Theory and Practice*, 37(3), 479–504.

Fletcher, D., Melin, L. and Gimeno, A. 2012. Culture and values in family business, *Journal of Family Business Strategy*, 3(3), 127–131.

Growing Inclusive Markets Initiative 2008. *Creating Value for All: Strategies for Doing Business With the Poor*, New York, NY, United Nations Development Programme.

Hanson, S.K., Hessel, H.M. and Danes, S.M. 2019. Relational processes in family entrepreneurial culture and resilience across generations, *Journal of Family Business Strategy*, 10(3). doi: 10.1016/j.jfbs.2018.11.001

London, T., Anupindi, R. and Sheth, S. 2010. Creating mutual value: lessons learned from ventures serving base of the pyramid producers, *Journal of Business Research*, 63(6), 582–594.

McMullen, J.S. and Dimov, D. 2013. Time and the entrepreneurial journey, *Journal of Management Studies*, 50(8), 1481–1512.

Oughton, P.D. and Wheelock, J. 2003. A capabilities approach to sustainable household livelihoods, *Review of Social Economy*, 61(1), 1–22.

Welter, F. 2011. Contextualizing entrepreneurship—conceptual challenges and ways forward, *Entrepreneurship: Theory and Practice*, 35(1), 165–184.

2

RETHINKING THE DYNAMICS OF MICRO ENTERPRISE: MOBILISING NECESSITY ENTREPRENEURSHIP FOR THE NEEDS OF DEPRIVED COMMUNITIES

INTRODUCTION

Micro enterprise is often synonymous with enterprise in deprived communities because it refers to ventures established for the purpose of providing livelihood to their founders. This is in contrast to ventures established to achieve innovation or promote special goods or services. Furthermore, enterprises established to provide livelihood or products and services fitting the needs of deprived communities are often associated with necessity entrepreneurship. This chapter investigates differences and similarities in concepts and terminology related to necessity and micro entrepreneurship. It also draws insights into the dynamics of micro enterprises in terms of the characteristics that might shape the enterprising culture in deprived communities and the role of necessity entrepreneurs in revitalising disadvantaged areas.

Micro enterprises are major providers of local products and services, as well as employment, as they tend to fill gaps in supply to the local areas. However, defining micro enterprise is not without challenges. Governing bodies tend to categorise micro enterprises using size as the main criterion. The Australian, Canadian and the US government authorities in charge of small business administration identify a micro enterprise as a trading entity that has less than five employees (Australian Bureau of Statistics, 2019; Industry Canada, 2019). The UK and EU policy makers lift the bar to 10 employees plus utilise a variable threshold on annual turnover (European Commission Recommendation 2003/361, 2003; Office for National Statistics, 2016). Adding the turnover criterion seems to be a sensible approach as otherwise a micro enterprise with four employees employing one or more extra people would change, from the government perspective, its status. However, typically there would not be any noticeable changes in the way this micro enterprise operates. Therefore, avoiding the size criterion is preferred. Rather, a micro enterprise should be viewed in a more holistic way taking into consideration the context in which necessity-driven entrepreneurially minded individuals engage in business activities.

WHAT IS NECESSITY ENTREPRENEURSHIP?

Necessity entrepreneurship represents a paradigm where a person engages in entrepreneurial activity because of a lack of employment choices and the need to ensure livelihood; therefore, an enterprise is established mainly for that purpose. Necessity entrepreneurship can be viewed as a cumulative category of small business founders, rather than a specific set of characteristics describing entrepreneurs of a certain type. Rehn and Taalas (2004) use the term *mundane* entrepreneurship to describe the situation when a person aims to secure a decent living for themself. Overall, there is an established view that necessity entrepreneurship reflects a *forced choice* when a person is pushed into self-employment because of an absence of alternatives (McMullen et al., 2008).

Another use of the term 'necessity entrepreneurship' can be found within the scope of the Global Entrepreneurship Monitor (GEM) project. Acs (2006) suggests distinguishing necessity entrepreneurs, or those individuals who become entrepreneurs because they have no better option, from opportunity-driven entrepreneurs who actively choose to start a new enterprise based on the perception that an unexploited or underexploited business opportunity exists. Elaborating on the findings of the GEM project, researchers indicate that necessity entrepreneurship is widespread in developing countries, principally because of the lack of suitable job opportunities (Reynolds et al., 2005). Irrespective of the underlying motives of necessity entrepreneurs, the GEM project's statistical analysis concluded that there is a strong positive relationship between necessity entrepreneurship and national economic growth. Furthermore, as necessity helps to turn the unemployed and jobseekers to self-employment, this makes necessity entrepreneurship implicitly relevant to the challenges facing many deprived communities. Therefore, the comment that 'government and non-government institutions may need to develop a different set of processes and policies for the support of necessity entrepreneurship' (Reynolds et al., 2005, p. 26) deserves full attention. Specifically, government support to developing enterprise culture, fostering necessity entrepreneurship, might be a key focus area of local governing bodies (Vasilieva et al., 2008).

THE ESSENCE OF NECESSITY ENTREPRENEURSHIP

An entrepreneur creates a new business out of necessity 'because all other options for work are either absent or unsatisfactory' (Acs, 2006, p. 98). More than half of all entrepreneurs in developing countries are 'pushed' into self-employment or entrepreneurship (Poschke, 2013; Puente et al., 2019). Having decided that no other income-generating activity or job opportunity is available, these individuals create a small business with a great deal of reluctance. Dawson and Henley (2012) refer to the conduct of such entrepreneurial activities as *push* entrepreneurship, while Fayolle (2011) labels it *forced* entrepreneurship. As a result, some individuals establish a new venture while, and despite, lacking self-confidence and skills (Mühlböck et al., 2018). They also experience additional difficulties owing to having either a negative perception of business opportunities or a lack of their understanding. While describing this style of new venture creation as a *desperate*, out of necessity act, Mühlböck et al. (2018) coin the term 'NONS entrepreneurs' in characterising necessity entrepreneurs, where NONS stands for 'No Opportunities No Skills'. In addition, for these individuals, who consider the labour market to be tight or unfavourable, self-employment appears to be an attractive option for generating income before making transition to a more remunerative activity.

Necessity entrepreneurs are often contrasted with opportunity entrepreneurs and are seen as the opposite of opportunity-driven entrepreneurs (Acs, 2006; Calderon et al., 2016; Mühlböck et al., 2018; van der Zwan et al., 2016). Unlike opportunity-driven entrepreneurs, who are pulled by a perceived market opportunity, necessity entrepreneurs are pushed into entrepreneurship even though they may not have the necessary skills and resources to run a business (Mühlböck et al., 2018). The push motivation suggests involuntary nature as one of key characteristics of necessity entrepreneurship.

There is, however, an opinion that the phenomenon of necessity entrepreneurship should not be linked to necessity only. Krueger and Brazeal (1994) insist that entrepreneurs are driven by the perceived desirability and feasibility of their enterprise. While necessity entrepreneurs may lack the passion typically exhibited by opportunity-driven entrepreneurs because of personal financial predicaments or unemployment, their decision to start a business is arguably also opportunity-driven. For necessity entrepreneurs, the decision to launch a venture is driven by market attractiveness and rationalisation of barriers to market entry, in addition to unemployment (Nikiforou et al., 2019). In this light, necessity entrepreneurs may also pursue a series of activities including cost–benefit analysis, market evaluation or perhaps risk assessment before launching a new product or service, just as any conventional entrepreneur would do. At the very least, they need to identify which target market to enter and evaluate whether the potential benefits outweigh the costs of running a business. In other words, the necessity entrepreneurs may also take calculated risks, just like opportunity-driven entrepreneurs.

It is worth noting that not every unemployed person, even when equipped with skills sufficient to establish and run a venture, chooses to engage in entrepreneurship out of necessity. This choice makes necessity entrepreneurs different from other unemployed individuals as they are willing to engage in entrepreneurial endeavours and undertake calculated risk. There is another pool of candidates potentially suited for necessity entrepreneurship, that is people in employment. From the perspective of the rational choice theory, individuals make rational decisions and choose a suitable course of action in line with their personal objectives and/or preferences. Drawing on the rational choice theory, Pfeiffer and Reize

(2000) argue that an individual will decide in favour of entrepreneurship if the perceived benefits exceed the current or expected benefits from permanent employment. The expectancy theory, on the other hand, suggests individuals choose to be entrepreneurs due to expectations about the outcomes of entrepreneurial activities. Expected outcomes presumably differ between necessity entrepreneurs and growth-oriented entrepreneurs. For necessity entrepreneurs, the ambition is quite straightforward and is less likely to include the intention to expand business operations (Mühlböck et al., 2018). These entrepreneurs expect to be financially independent, at least for a short while (Dawson and Henley, 2012).

IMPACT OF A RESOURCE-STARVED ENVIRONMENT ON NECESSITY ENTREPRENEURS

Deprived areas are often described as having a resource-starved environment, which may force or enable necessity entrepreneurs to mobilise resources more creatively in order to make a living. These individuals, who mostly originate from the 'bottom of the pyramid' (BoP), are forced to redefine or challenge the concept of resource availability. Thus, they are well positioned to use their ingenuity and persistence to acquire or redefine the resources necessary to build up their enterprises (Diomande, 1990).

Ludwick Marishane is a shining example of an entrepreneur whose efforts and diligence overcame resource constraints and produced an ingenious product uniquely suited for the needs of the 'BoP' population in Africa and beyond. He invented and perfected over time DryBath, a waterless bathing solution, helping to fight hygiene-related diseases, such as trachoma, and the ability to stay clean in a dry and water-deprived climate. Trachoma, an eye infection resulting from dirt getting into the eyes, affects hundreds of millions of children in Africa and leaves many permanently blind every year. The treatment of trachoma is simple – the face needs to be washed with water. The idea was driven by a hygiene-related problem affecting a very large number of children (Marishane, 2012). By being persistent, the desired outcome was achieved, i.e. a successful product was created. Ludwick spent years researching, testing, perfecting the product and raising money. The initial bulk of the work was done on a basic Nokia phone, without computers and almost without any Internet connectivity. And when the product was perfected, Ludwick did not stop. He continued until he matched it to the needs of both the curiosity-driven market – students and other interested people – and the BoP audience who could only afford to pay for one DryBath at a time.

Ludwick Marishane does not completely fit the typical path of necessity entrepreneurs because he was more driven by the need to solve the water shortage problem rather than by overcoming his inability to gain employment. However, it seems that the old adage 'necessity is the mother of invention' still applies to the case of DryBath founder.

Analysing the role of resource deprivation as a determinant of necessity entrepreneurship might shed light on whether necessity is the source of creativity and innovation. A good example of that is Moses Kizza Musaazi, a necessity-driven innovator. He invented the Interlocking Soil Stabilised Brick that serves as a cost-effective building material using soil and other ingredients available in the local area. His interlocking soil bricks are now commonly used in schools and homes all over Uganda and brick-making has become an alternative revenue stream for local schools (Royal Academy of Engineering, 2019).

Another distinctive example is SolarTurtle (www.solarturtle.co.za), a company established to support local entrepreneurs by offering portable battery recharging services to rural communities in Africa, using a franchise model, in which local women are trained to promote and run these small energy franchises (Royal Academy of Engineering, 2019). These entrepreneurs, also known as 'turtlepreneurs' because of the resemblance of community-owned solar kiosks to turtles, are trained to sell electricity and energy-efficient devices and also encouraged to add their own ventures to the newly electrified facilities. These entrepreneurs understand the everyday challenges faced by underserved communities and offer affordable solutions to overcome those challenges.

It is important to point out that the abovementioned innovators are recipients of various awards and grants. Ludwick Marishane received a USD 10,000 cash prize for winning Global Student Entrepreneur Awards in 2011 and used the prize money to develop DryBath. Co-funded by the European Commission, SolarTurtle received EUR 355,382 to build the solar kiosk model of generating off-grid renewable energy in the Thaba-Tseka district in Lesotho (European Commission, 2019). One could argue these entrepreneurship stories would be very different without the financial support provided by external parties. Access to finance is an essential condition for new venture creation; this is always cited as a major challenge for deprived communities (Fuentelsaz et al., 2015).

In the absence of, or having acute shortage of, start-up capital, deprived communities in low- and middle-income countries engage in *micro-trade,* such as street vending, hawking and small retail businesses (Lyons et al., 2014). These micro enterprises are often associated with smaller growth expectations and less innovation compared to opportunity entrepreneurship (Mühlböck et al., 2018). Financially deprived communities are not a homogenous group; some of them may exhibit more passion and effort than others (Banerjee and Duflo, 2011). Although there are successful examples of entrepreneurship originating at the BoP, many micro enterprises that are driven by desperation and necessity are 'doomed to remain small and unprofitable' (Banerjee and Duflo, 2011, p. 225).

Often unemployment per se (i.e. lack of economic activity) is not a problem for unemployed individuals; loss of income and poverty that come with unemployment are the life-ruining problems. Banerjee and Duflo (2011, p. 226) conclude that 'perhaps the many businesses of the poor are less a testimony to their entrepreneurial spirit than a symptom of the dramatic failure of the economies in which they live to provide them with something better'.

INSTITUTIONAL SUPPORT FOR MICRO ENTERPRISES

A mounting body of entrepreneurship research has explored the effects of country-specific institutional arrangements on entrepreneurship (Fuentelsaz et al., 2015; Puente et al., 2019). Institutional theorists (Baumol, 1990; Williams, 2008; Walter and Block, 2016) assert that the institutional environment can strongly influence the development of entrepreneurship. Bruton et al. (2010) suggested that the socio-cultural environment determines individual decision to become entrepreneurs. From a macro perspective, not all types of entrepreneurship contribute productively to societies and economies (Mühlböck et al., 2018). Institutional settings in a country influence not only the perception and orientation of entrepreneurs towards wealth creation activities (Baumol, 1990) but also the extent to which their entrepreneurial endeavours are productive for society (Bruton et al., 2010).

Institutional and economic circumstances serve as either push or pull factors for entrepreneurship and can be considered together with the argument in support of prosperity-pull and recession-led entrepreneurship. According to the 'pull' hypothesis, favourable institutional aspects (e.g. low levels of risk and high levels of ease in business creation) act as pull factors which encourage people to become entrepreneurs. On the other hand, push factors, such as an economic downturn (Mühlböck et al., 2018) and low labour freedom (Fuentelsaz et al., 2015), reduce the prospects of finding paid jobs and thus push people to be self-employed or to create a small business (Nikiforou et al., 2019) due to an expectation that the returns of entrepreneurship could be greater than those of unemployment.

Earlier entrepreneurship research has explored a range of economic and legal institutional factors that affect entry into entrepreneurship. These include taxation (Belitski et al., 2016), industry wage levels (Nikiforou et al., 2019), employment law (Stel et al., 2007), entry regulations (Lyon et al., 2014) and property rights protection (Baumol, 1990). Studies have also explored the effect of corruption at a national level on entrepreneurship, with some researchers concluding that better control of corruption is associated with rising levels of innovation and entrepreneurial activity (Anokhin and Schulze, 2009; Dutta and Sobel, 2016), while Walter and Block (2016) found that control of corruption was significantly negatively related to entrepreneurship. Interestingly, Belitski et al. (2016) found that corruption can offset the negative influences of high taxes on entry.

The dynamics of the institutional environment partially define, or shape, necessity entrepreneurship. Institutional support is often needed to protect both consumer and producer interests. Institutions, such as licensing, guarantees and industry watchdogs, form some of the common practices overcoming market uncertainty caused by information asymmetry (Sarasvathy et al., 2010). An illustrative example of institutional support is the bKash company inspired and launched in 2011 by Kamal Quadir with the help of BRAC Bank Limited, focusing on providing services to small and medium-sized enterprises in Bangladesh. bKash (www.bkash.com) provides financial services through a network of community-based agents using mobile phone technology (Yesmin et al., 2019). The company aims to service the poor who have limited access to formal banking services. Relying on the help of micro entrepreneurs in urban and rural areas in much of Bangladesh, it quickly grew to serve 22% of the population in 2013 (Chen and Rasmussen, 2014). Today, bKash is the largest provider of mobile financial services in Bangladesh.

However, an absence of institutional support creates market uncertainty and even shapes an entrepreneurship-hostile environment. In places like Durban and Cape Town, street vending is either absent or confined to a restricted area. Street vendors in Durban, for instance, have been denied permits for decades without answers or updates from the local authorities (Xolo, 2018). Government gives fines to unlicensed traders, evicts them and confiscates their inventories (Lyon et al., 2014), which further worsens the situation of already deprived communities and diminishes any hopes of upward social mobility. Such entrepreneurship-hostile institutions are likely to encourage informal entrepreneurship that is driven by necessity and opportunity (Williams, 2008).

INFORMAL ECONOMY

Government policies that eliminate administrative rigidities allow entrepreneurs to compete freely in an open market. In contrast, countries with excessive administrative burdens requiring registration and licensing of new ventures discourage formal registration and often lead entrepreneurs to operate informally. Informal entrepreneurs are viewed as unregistered businesses as well as 'registered enterprises but conducting a portion of their trade off-the-books' (Williams, 2008, p. 161). These businesses range from unlicensed street hawkers to drug dealers. Because of the unregistered nature of the informal economy, it is difficult to quantify the exact number of informal enterprises.

Informal entrepreneurship is more complex than the *necessity vs opportunistic* duality of entrepreneurial motivation. Furthermore, it should be noted that entrepreneurial motivation does not remain constant over time. It fluctuates beyond the realms of necessity and opportunity, driven by a multiplicity of factors, such as relationships with friends and family, local events and news. This line of thinking leads to another pertinent question: when and where should we draw a line between a potential entrepreneur and non-entrepreneur in a less formal sense? Can we refer to individuals who have not commercialised a market opportunity formally (by establishing a venture) as entrepreneurs? Puente et al. (2019) suggest that we need to consider another notion of *transition entrepreneurship*, referring to individuals who wish to start a business but cannot yet quit their day jobs. Such 'part time' entrepreneurs, while still in transition, may be stuck in a situation of having a job and getting involved in an informal enterprise.

DEPRIVED COMMUNITIES AND THE BOTTOM OF THE PYRAMID

The notion of necessity is closely associated with desperation and deprivation. Prahalad and Hammond (2002) used the term 'the bottom of the pyramid' to describe a large number of people living in extreme poverty, typically earning and living on less than a few US dollars per day, having limited access to water, food, energy, education and transportation. Constrained by scarce resources, those who are at the bottom of the wealth hierarchy are likely to be unemployed and represent an underutilised labour force and untapped consumer power at the same time (Dolan and Roll, 2013). BoP literature has been devoted to exploring ways of developing these lower levels of income, transforming the ignored or unproductive labour force and overlooked consumers into a viable market for capital mobilisation. One such undertaking is the collaboration of Grameenphone and Grameen Bank, envisaged by Iqbal Quadir, an entrepreneur and a passionate proponent of entrepreneurship for bringing prosperity to low-income communities. This initiative has been targeting the vast numbers of BoP population in Bangladesh.

Grameenphone, the leading telecommunications service provider in Bangladesh, provides women entrepreneurs known as 'phone ladies' in rural villages with a regular mobile phone and a solar recharger; the average cost of $175 is financed by the means of a micro-loan model introduced by Grameen Bank. The phone ladies aim to provide phone services to people in their own villages, who pay per call rather than incurring the extensive costs of owning a phone – contract and maintenance fees.

This innovative idea provided by the entrepreneur to geographically distributed necessity entrepreneurs in deprived areas allowed the improvement of the quality of life of large masses of BoP population. In a few years of running, it generated a widespread service provided through around 75,000 phone ladies who have a supplementary income of approximately $1,000 per year, while per capita income in Bangladesh is $286 per year (Simanis and Hart, 2006), and ensuring access to telecommunication services to half of

Bangladesh's rural population. Because of its positive impact on BoP population, this enterprising model has been replicated in some African countries, namely Uganda and Rwanda.

To sum up, the institutional environment and the socio-cultural context of BoP are essential for facilitating micro enterprise and overcoming numerous challenges. Among these are the availability of limited start-up capital or even no start-up capital; an uneducated workforce; dominance of informal governance mechanisms (Dolan and Roll, 2013); high levels of uncertainty; and absent or inadequate infrastructure (Simanis and Hart, 2006). Necessity or BoP entrepreneurs wishing to tap in the BoP market need to be equipped with both an understanding of these challenges and strategies to overcome these.

DEPRIVED COMMUNITIES IN INDUSTRIALISED ECONOMIES

In contrast, deprived areas in developed countries face a slightly different set of constraints. Williams and Williams (2011), in a study of enterprise development policy for stimulating entrepreneurship in deprived urban neighbourhoods of Leeds, found that individuals living in underserviced areas have their entrepreneurial endeavour limited by a range of barriers that can be divided in two groups – direct and indirect. The direct constraints are represented by lack of self-belief and confidence and lack of affordable workspace, while indirect barriers are shaped by individual beliefs, such as perceptions of place, fear of crime and financial lending hurdles.

Similarly, in an analysis of GEM data for Scotland, Levie (2011) found that the low levels of entrepreneurial activity identified in deprived local areas are not due to the lack of interest in entrepreneurship but because aspirations are not translated into action. It seems that the mentality of people living in deprived localities is not supportive of business creation and ownership, with the controlling factor being grounded in personal background that is often characterised by an underdeveloped enterprise culture. This deeply embedded predisposition to pass up market opportunities, complemented by the difficulties of obtaining start-up funds and inability to tap into family and friends' financial resources, produce a snowball effect affecting generations of people who do not even consider the path of entrepreneurship.

In summary, while some deprived communities demonstrate the situation expressed by the proverbial saying that 'not everyone can be an entrepreneur', some others have developed a mindset portrayed by the proverbial variation that 'not everyone wants to be an entrepreneur'.

The preceding discussion identified four main types of necessity entrepreneurship: NONS, informal, transition, and necessity-inspired entrepreneurship. These four types have different levels of formality and growth potential, as Fig. 2.1 shows.

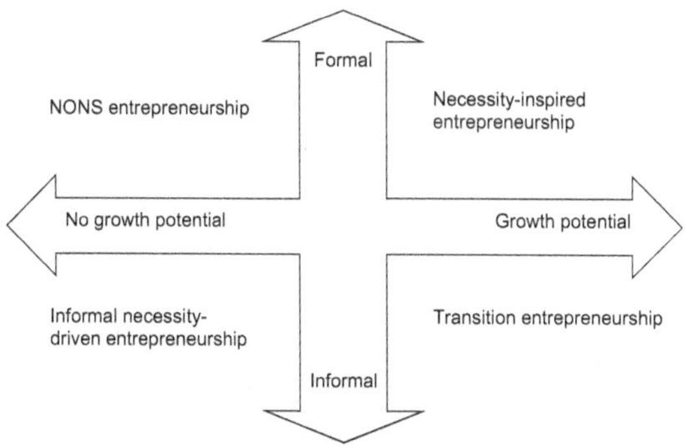

Fig. 2.1. Typology of Necessity Entrepreneurship.

Necessity-inspired entrepreneurship – this type of entrepreneur is inspired by daily necessity, comes up with a solution to solve everyday problems and commercialises the idea. SolarTurtle and DryBath are good examples of this.

Transition entrepreneurship – this type of entrepreneur is at a transition stage between an employee and entrepreneur. They tend to be growth-oriented, innovative, novice entrepreneurs. They possibly have not yet registered their business since they are in the process of contemplation of how to commercialise their business opportunities.

Informal necessity-driven entrepreneurship – this type of entrepreneurship includes unregistered retailers, street vendors, hawkers and also registered businesses that keep part of their business activities off the book.

NONS entrepreneurship – 'No Opportunity No Skills' entrepreneurship refers to early stage entrepreneurs 'who see either no opportunities, do not believe in their own skills, or both' (Mühlböck et al., 2018, p. 976). They prefer to work alone, probably with help from their family (Banerjee and Duflo, 2011) but remain small.

THE LANDSCAPE OF RESEARCH INTO NECESSITY ENTREPRENEURSHIP

While some research has relied on single-country data to link unemployment and necessity entrepreneurship (Pfeiffer and Reize, 2000; Dawson and Henley, 2012; Block et al., 2015; Calderon et al., 2016; Nikiforou et al., 2019), the majority of studies use cross-country data or time-series analysis to study necessity entrepreneurship (Acs, 2006; Williams, 2008; Poschke, 2013; Fuentelsaz et al., 2015; Walter and Block, 2016; van der Zwan et al., 2016; Mühlböck et al., 2018; Puente et al., 2019). Table 2.1 summarises the findings within a broad theme of necessity entrepreneurship.

Most empirical research conducted into necessity entrepreneurship used descriptive analysis based on the GEM survey or official statistics published by national governments. Most of these studies compared necessity entrepreneurship with opportunity entrepreneurship and draw similar conclusions; that is, opportunity entrepreneurship outperforms necessity entrepreneurship (Acs, 2006; Pfeiffer and Reize, 2000; van der Zwan et al., 2016) and necessity entrepreneurs require further training (Calderon et al., 2016; Mühlböck et al., 2018; Nikiforou et al., 2019). For example, a study published by the World Bank Group concluded that financial performance of opportunity entrepreneurship is significantly better than that of businesses led by necessity entrepreneurs, partly due to better management practices (Calderon et al., 2016). Studies also showed that necessity entrepreneurs are more likely to encounter business failure than opportunity entrepreneurs (Pfeiffer and Reize, 2000; van der Zwan et al., 2016).

Poschke (2013) characterised necessity entrepreneurship in terms of socio-economic variables. Based on GEM data collected between 2001 and 2005, the analysis reveals that necessity entrepreneurs have lower education levels, run smaller firms and generally do not expect their firms to grow. In a similar vein, van der Zwan et al. (2016) found significant differences between opportunity and necessity entrepreneurs in terms of socio-demographic characteristics and entrepreneurial perceptions. Based on data collected by Euro-Barometer and Gallup, van der Zwan et al. (2016) reported that necessity entrepreneurs are more likely to be female, financially disadvantaged and pessimistic. It is worth noting that the gender factor in necessity entrepreneurship is debatable because other studies found no significant gender

Table 2.1. Studies of Necessity Entrepreneurship: Methodology and Findings.

Author	Methods	Data Source	No. of Countries	Findings
Pfeiffer and Reize (2000)	Survey; time series analysis	ZEW Firm Startup Panel	1; Germany	Firm survival is negatively affected by foundation from unemployment
Bygrave et al. (2003)	Survey; interview; regression analysis	GEM	29	Necessity-pushed entrepreneurship does not correlate with opportunity perception, skills and experience, and informal investment
Maritz (2004)	Survey	GEM	1; New Zealand	New Zealand's high necessity entrepreneurial level is characterised by low unemployment levels and generous welfare benefits
Reynolds et al. (2005)	Survey; time series analysis	GEM	41	One-third of GEM respondents indicate they are acting out of necessity; there is substantial variation across countries in these proportions

Acs (2006)	Survey	GEM	39	The opportunity–necessity ratio is used as a composite indicator of entrepreneurial activity and economic development
Bergmann and Sternberg (2007)	Survey; regression analysis	GEM	1; Germany	Increasing levels of unemployment in Germany contribute to the increase in the number of necessity start-ups
Williams (2008)	Case study; interview	Maximum variation sampling method	3; United Kingdom; Ukraine; Russia	Two-thirds of respondents start out as necessity-orientated, then turn into opportunity-orientated entrepreneurs
Block and Koellinger (2009)	Survey; univariate and multivariate analysis	Subscribers of the newsletter 'news2use'	1; Germany	Necessity entrepreneurs are unhappy because of the lack of viable options, which explains the loss of experienced utility and satisfaction
Kautonen and Palmroos (2010)	Survey; regression analysis	Statistics Finland	1; Finland	Necessity entrepreneurship has a significant negative effect on the desire to continue in self-employment

Table 2.1. (*Continued*)

Author	Methods	Data Source	No. of Countries	Findings
Dawson and Henley (2012)	Survey; time series analysis	UK Quarterly Labour Force Survey	1; United Kingdom	The most popular reason given for both men and women to start a business is 'independence'
Poschke (2013)	Survey	GEM	36	Necessity entrepreneurs are less educated than opportunity entrepreneurs
Fuentelsaz et al. (2015)	Survey; time series analysis	GEM	63	Increased development of formal institutions favours opportunity entrepreneurship
Block et al. (2015)	Survey	KfW/ZEW Start-up Panel	1; Germany	Necessity entrepreneurs are more likely to pursue a cost leadership strategy than differentiation strategy
Walter and Block (2016)	Survey; interview; multilevel analysis	Flash Eurobarometer	36	The outcomes of entrepreneurship education are contingent on a country's institutional environment

van der Zwan et al. (2016)	Survey; interview; cross sectional analysis	Flash Eurobarometer; Gallup	33	The probability of being an opportunity vs a necessity business owner is higher for male, younger, wealthier, proactive and optimistic business owners
Calderon et al. (2016)	Survey; cross-sectional analysis	Census data; Mexican Statistical Institute	1; Mexico	Necessity entrepreneurship is less profitable than opportunity entrepreneurship
Mühlböck et al. (2018)	Survey; time series analysis	GEM	17	People started a business despite a negative perception of business opportunities as well as lack of confidence in their own entrepreneurial skills
Nikiforou et al. (2019)	Interview; survey; multivariate analyses	Greek Statistical Office; Independent Authority for Public Revenue	1; Greece	The level of need (or necessity) is not uniform and it increases with time spent in unemployment
Puente et al. (2019)	Survey; time series analysis	GEM	6; Latin America	Some necessity entrepreneurs in Latin America aspire to grow

differences between necessity entrepreneurs (Pfeiffer and Reize, 2000; Poschke, 2013) and some researchers even found that men are more likely to be necessity entrepreneurs. Based on a UK sample, Dawson and Henley (2012) found that men are more likely to be pushed into entrepreneurship by unemployment or lack of job opportunities. It thus appears that profiling necessity entrepreneurship based on socio-demographic factors is somewhat futile. Rather, it is the perception of necessity entrepreneurs that makes them different from other strands of entrepreneurship. As Bergmann and Sternberg (2007, p. 219) summarise it: 'These start-ups for lack of alternative employment opportunities are predominantly launched independently of the entrepreneurs' age, gender, level of education and regional influences, due to the individual's perception of a situation of economic need'.

CONCLUSION

Across the globe, the decision to start a new business is influenced by varying factors. Entrepreneurship researchers suggest that necessity entrepreneurs are largely motivated by unemployment, rather by the desire to exploit a market opportunity. Arguably, however, unemployment alone does not motivate one to become an entrepreneur.

Researchers typically assumed that necessity entrepreneurs are motivated by financial factors and pushed people into new venture creation (Acs, 2006; Mühlböck et al., 2018; Calderon et al., 2016; van der Zwan et al., 2016). However, necessity entrepreneurs may be also pulled by market attractiveness or perceived earnings, in addition to the long-held belief that they are entrepreneurs out of necessity. The decision to enter a particular market is largely based on its perceived feasibility and desirability (Krueger and Brazeal, 1994). As Dawson and Henley (2012) stated, entrepreneurship becomes relatively attractive either because perceived earnings from employment have fallen or discontinued (push), or perceived returns on investment are greater than current earnings or unemployment (pull), or a combination of both factors. Distinguishing entrepreneurship based on motivation (e.g. push vs pull; growth vs lifestyle; necessity vs opportunity) is therefore incomplete or even misleading.

After consolidation of all identified characteristics of micro enterprising into the enterprise culture model the following balance emerges. The factors stimulating entrepreneurial activities in deprived communities are scarce but include institutional support and availability of funding. The factors hindering entrepreneurship in deprived areas are awareness of or lack of it in estimating risks; lack of training and overall preparedness to launch and then manage a venture; and lack of self-confidence complicated by having either negative perceptions or lack of understanding of market opportunities. This rather unsettling list of barriers to engaging in entrepreneurial activities indicates the dominance of push motivations for necessity entrepreneurship suggesting an involuntary or reluctant nature as one of key characteristics of micro enterprising.

LEARNING POINTS

- Local governing bodies might be in the position to leverage micro enterprise creation by focusing on the factors stimulating entrepreneurship. These might include training on new venture creation and business planning, skill building training programmes, streamlining institutional procedures for issuing business licences and permits, partnering with NGOs regarding micro grant making for new enterprise creation and promoting best micro enterprise practice in deprived communities by advertising and local events. These activities need to feed in the overarching objective – to shift the mindset of prospective entrepreneurs. Rather than driven by a necessity, micro enterprise formation could be fostered by the entrepreneurial aspiration and supported by the favourable local context.

- Market attractiveness and venture's feasibility need to be explained to prospective entrepreneurs to move their thinking from necessity to desirability. This would permit to avoid overestimation of risk, costs and complexity of micro enterprise creation and promote calculated and planned small ventures' launch.
- As many people are passionate and caring about the-community where they live, local governing bodies, together with other interested parties, should emphasise contribution of micro entrepreneurship to the local area development. This might serve as an additional – and quite powerful – factor stimulating micro entrepreneurship, leading to building pride in the local community engagement.

REFERENCES

Acs, Z. 2006. How is entrepreneurship good for economic growth? *Innovations*, 1(1), 97–107.

Anokhin, S. and Schulze, W.S. 2009. Entrepreneurship, innovation, and corruption. *Journal of Business Venturing*, 24(5), 465–476.

Australian Bureau of Statistics. 2019. *Business Performance by Size*. Available at: https://www.abs.gov.au/ausstats/abs@.nsf/Latestproducts/8155.0Main%20Features42017-18?opendocument&tabname=Summary&prodno=8155.0&issue=2017-18&num=&view=

Banerjee, A.V. and Duflo, E. 2011. *Poor Economics: A Radical Rethinking of the Way to Fight Global Poverty*, New York, NY, Public Affairs Press.

Baumol, W.J. 1990. Entrepreneurship: productive, unproductive, and destructive. *Journal of Political Economy*, 98(5), 893–921.

Belitski, M., Chowdhury, F. and Desai, S. 2016. Taxes, corruption, and entry. *Small Business Economics*, 47(1), 201–216.

Bergmann, H. and Sternberg, R. 2007. The changing face of entrepreneurship in Germany. *Small Business Economics*, 28(2–3), 205–221.

Block, J. and Koellinger, P. 2009. I can't get no satisfaction—necessity entrepreneurship and procedural utility. *Kyklos*, 62(2), 191–209.

Block, J.H., Kohn, K., Miller, D. and Ullrich, K. 2015. Necessity entrepreneurship and competitive strategy. *Small Business Economics*, 44(1), 37–54.

Bruton, G.D., Ahlstrom, D. and Li, H.L. 2010. Institutional theory and entrepreneurship: where are we now and where do we need to move in the future? *Entrepreneurship: Theory and Practice*, 34(3), 421–440.

Bygrave, W., Hay, M., Ng, E. and Reynolds, P. 2003. Executive forum: a study of informal investing in 29 nations composing the Global Entrepreneurship Monitor. *Venture Capital*, 5(2), 101–116.

Calderon, G., Iacovone, L. and Juarez, L. 2016. *Opportunity versus Necessity: Understanding the Heterogeneity of Female Micro-Entrepreneurs*, Washington, DC, The World Bank Group.

Chen, G. and Rasmussen, S. 2014. *bKash Bangladesh: A Fast Start for Mobile Financial Services*, Washington, DC, World Bank. Available at: https://openknowledge.worldbank.org/bitstream/handle/10986/20262/909520BRI0Box30Bangladesh0July02014.pdf?sequence=1

Dawson, C. and Henley, A. 2012. Push versus pull entrepreneurship: an ambiguous distinction. *International Journal of Entrepreneurial Behaviour & Research*, 18(6), 697–719.

Diomande, M. 1990. Business creation with minimal resources: some lessons from the African experience. *Journal of Business Venturing*, 5(4), 191–200.

Dolan, C. and Roll, K. 2013. Capital's new frontier: from "unusable" economies to bottom-of-the-pyramid markets in Africa. *African Studies Review*, 56(3), 123–146.

Dutta, N. and Sobel, R. 2016. Does corruption ever help entrepreneurship? *Small Business Economics*, 47(1), 179–199.

European Commission. 2019. *Renewable Energy Women Empowerment Project (REWEP)*. Available at: https://eeas.europa.eu/csdp-missions-operations/eutm-rca/60306/renewable-energy-women-empowerment-project-rewep_fr

European Commission. 2003. Recommendation 2003/361 on the definition of micro, small and medium-sized enterprises. *Official Journal of the European Union*, L124, 36–41.

Fayolle, A. 2011. Necessity entrepreneurship and job insecurity: the hidden face of entrepreneurship. *International Journal of E-Entrepreneurship and Innovation*, 2(3), 1–10.

Fuentelsaz, L., González, C., Maícas, J.P. and Montero, J. 2015. How different formal institutions affect opportunity and necessity entrepreneurship. *BRQ Business Research Quarterly*, 18(4), 246–258.

Industry Canada. 2019. *Key Small Business Statistics – January 2019*. Available at: https://www.ic.gc.ca/eic/site/061.nsf/eng/h_03090.html

Kautonen, T. and Palmroos, J. 2010. The impact of a necessity-based start-up on subsequent entrepreneurial satisfaction. *The International Entrepreneurship and Management Journal*, 6(3), 285–300.

Krueger, N.F. and Brazeal, D.V. 1994. Entrepreneurial potential and potential entrepreneurs. *Entrepreneurship: Theory and Practice*, 18(3), 91–104.

Levie, J. 2011. *Global Entrepreneurship Monitor Scotland 2011*, Scotland, GEM Consortium. Available at: https://www.strath.ac.uk/media/departments/huntercentre/research/gem/GEM_Scotland_2011.pdf

Lyons, M., Brown, A. and Msoka, C. 2014. Do micro enterprises benefit from the 'Doing Business' reforms? The case of street-vending in Tanzania. *Urban Studies*, 51(8), 1593–1612.

Marishane, L. 2012. *Ludwick Marishane: A Bath without Water*. [Video file]. Available at: https://www.ted.com/talks/ludwick_marishane_a_bath_without_water?language=en [Accessed 12 September 2019].

Maritz, A. 2004. Tri-nations entrepreneurial scorecard. *International Journal of Entrepreneurship and Small Business*, 1(3/4), 230–237.

McMullen, J.S., Bagby, D.R. and Palich, L.E. 2008. Economic freedom and the motivation to engage in entrepreneurial action. *Entrepreneurship: Theory and Practice*, 32(5), 875–895.

Mühlböck, M., Warmuth, J.R., Holienka, M. and Kittel, B. 2018. Desperate entrepreneurs: no opportunities, no skills. *The International Entrepreneurship and Management Journal*, 14(4), 975–997.

Nikiforou, A., Dencker, J.C. and Gruber, M. 2019. Necessity entrepreneurship and industry choice in new firm creation. *Strategic Management Journal*, 40, 1–26. doi:10.1002/smj.3075

Office for National Statistics. 2016. *Micro Businesses*. Available at: https://www.ons.gov.uk/aboutus/transparencyandgovernance/freedomofinformationfoi/microbusinesses

Pfeiffer, F. and Reize, F. 2000. Business start-ups by the unemployed—an econometric analysis based on firm data. *Labour Economics*, 7(5), 629–663.

Poschke, M. 2013. Entrepreneurs out of necessity: a snapshot. *Applied Economics Letters*, 20(7), 658–663.

Prahalad, C.K. and Hammond, A. 2002. Serving the world's poor, profitably. *Harvard Business Review*, 80(9), 48–57.

Puente, E., Espitia, C.G. and Cervilla, M.A. 2019. Necessity entrepreneurship in Latin America: it is not that simple. *Entrepreneurship & Regional Development*, 31, 953–983. doi:10.1080/08985626.2019.1650294

Rehn, A. and Taalas, S. 2004. 'Znakomstva I Svyazi' (Acquaintances and connections) - Blat, the Soviet Union, and mundane entrepreneurship. *Entrepreneurship & Regional Development*, 16(3), 235–250.

Reynolds, P., Bosma, N., Autio, E., Hunt, S., De Bono, N., Servais, I., López-García, P. and Chin, N. 2005. Global entrepreneurship monitor: data collection design and implementation 1998–2003. *Small Business Economics*, 24(3), 205–231.

Royal Academy of Engineering. 2019. *The Africa Prize for Engineering Innovation: Five Years of the Africa Prize.* Available at: https://www.raeng.org.uk/publications/other/africa-prize-5-year-anniversary-book

Sarasvathy, S.D., Dew, N., Velamuri, S.R. and Venkataraman, S. 2010. Three views of entrepreneurial opportunity. In *Handbook of Entrepreneurship Research*, Eds Z. Acs and D.B. Audretsch, pp. 77–96, New York, NY, Springer.

Simanis, E. and Hart, S. 2006. Expanding possibilities at the base of the pyramid. *Innovations: Technology, Governance, Globalization*, 1(1), 43–51.

Stel, A., Storey, D. and Thurik, A. 2007. The effect of business regulations on nascent and young business entrepreneurship. *Small Business Economics*, 28(2/3), 171–186.

Vasilieva, E., Avramenko, A., Heinze, A., MacLean, C., Rouse, J. and Crompton, H. 2008. *Building Bridges: Manchester Salford Enterprise Initiative: Enterprise Support and Engagement in Deprived Communities Pilots*, Salford, University of Salford.

Walter, S. and Block, J. 2016. Outcomes of entrepreneurship education: an institutional perspective. *Journal of Business Venturing*, 31(2), 216–233.

Williams, C.C. 2008. Beyond necessity-driven versus opportunity-driven entrepreneurship: a study of informal entrepreneurs in England, Russia and Ukraine. *The International Journal of Entrepreneurship and Innovation*, 9(3), 157–165.

Williams, N. and Williams, C.C. 2011. Tackling barriers to entrepreneurship in a deprived urban neighbourhood. *Local Economy*, 26(1), 30–42.

Xolo, N. 2018. Durban's informal traders march over by-law changes, GroundUp. Available at: http://www.groundup.org.za/article/informal-traders-march-over-law-amendments/

Yesmin S., Paul, T.A. and Mohshin Uddin, M. 2019. bKash: revolutionizing mobile financial services in Bangladesh? In *Business and Management Practices in South Asia*, EdsA. Sikdar and V. Pereira, pp. 125–148, Singapore, Palgrave Macmillan.

van der Zwan, P., Thurik, R., Verheul, I. and Hessels, J. 2016. Factors influencing the entrepreneurial engagement of opportunity and necessity entrepreneurs. *Eurasian Business Review*, 6(3), 273–295.

3

RURAL ENTREPRENEURSHIP

INTRODUCTION

Rural entrepreneurship has been attracting the attention of governments, local authorities, researchers and nascent and experienced entrepreneurs mainly due to the perception that competition is less intense in rural areas and there is a relatively large number of such areas in multiple countries. In many ways, rural areas and deprived communities have many commonalities: both can be characterised by low-income population, limited employment opportunities, a need for revitalisation and, often, higher crime rates. These similarities allow the rural entrepreneurship framework (discussed in this chapter) to be transposed to deprived communities, keeping in mind the lack of in-depth studies of entrepreneurship in deprived areas and aiming to contribute to the body of knowledge about enterprise in disadvantaged localities.

Entrepreneurship is a diverse social phenomenon that lacks a commonly accepted definition. Owing to this, the studies of rural entrepreneurship have been guided by various academic disciplines aiming largely to address social concerns, such as migration (Kalantaridis and Bika, 2006) and unemployment

(Möller, 2012). The field of rural entrepreneurship offers two principal approaches: the market-based view (Anthopoulou, 2010; Kordel, 2016; Hjalager and Kwiatkowski, 2018) and the resource-based view (Kalantaridis and Bika, 2006; Mitchell and Madden, 2014; Webster, 2017). The market demand perspective revolves around defining the nature and characteristics of rural entrepreneurship, whereas the resource-based view focuses on the methods used by rural entrepreneurs to mobilise scarce resources and their ability to do so.

From the market-based perspective, rural entrepreneurship is ultimately driven by market forces of supply and demand, i.e. rural entrepreneurs engage in business activities that aim to satisfy certain demand. The resource-based view explains entrepreneurship heterogeneity in the light of differences between entrepreneurs in their capability to mobilise resources and align with changes in the rural areas. The entrepreneurs' failure to do this often leads to a decline in the vitality of rural communities (Li et al., 2019). It is worth noting that the market-based and resource-based views are not mutually exclusive. The decision to create a new venture may be driven by both market pull and resource push. There is also a degree of conceptual overlap between rural and necessity entrepreneurship because the latter is mostly seen as an alternative to unemployment (Möller, 2012). Of course, almost any kind of entrepreneurship could be viewed as an alternative to unemployment in any setting including rural conditions, although often unemployment drives creation of small and micro enterprises with a limited capacity to expand their business operations.

Korsgaard et al. (2015, p. 5) argue that rural entrepreneurship as 'entrepreneurial activities that leverage local resources to re-connect place to space' should not be confused with entrepreneurship in rural areas because the latter represents 'entrepreneurial activities with limited embeddedness enacting a profit-oriented and mobile logic of space'. This argument emphasises the importance of understanding certain differences regarding space and place in entrepreneurial activities.

To sum up, rural entrepreneurs are not a homogeneous group, especially in an increasingly globalised economy influenced by in-migration, multiculturalism, the rise of digital natives in employment and other demographic changes in the rural population or in sparsely populated areas. Owing to this reason, when looking at rural entrepreneurship, it is necessary to 'assess why similar structural conditions are associated with dissimilar behavioural orientations' (Hoggart, 1990, p. 254).

RURALITY

To better understand rural entrepreneurship, it is important to look at the concept of *rurality* as it forms the basis of the entrepreneurial mindset and behaviour in rural areas. The discussion of rurality also adds to a growing debate on the definition of entrepreneurship in general and rural entrepreneurship in particular.

Central to understanding rurality are geographical remoteness and social order (Hoggart, 1990; Halfacree, 2007; Somerville et al., 2015). A community can be considered rural based on the following criteria: low population density, little or no spatial mobility, geographical remoteness, and insignificant social differentiation.

Rural entrepreneurs face logistics and financial challenges when they enter a certain market. Although recent technological innovations have significantly shortened the distance between a city and a village, the definition of rurality is not limited to a 'particular kind of geographical milieu' (Hoggart,

1990, p. 246). Rather, rurality applies to actions and inactions within a community, which partly contribute to the urban–rural divide. For example, most rural entrepreneurs engage in industries that are related to the land or natural amenities, which are viewed as rather uncommon by urban entrepreneurs.

The perception or image of rurality affects population migration behaviour (Van Dam et al., 2002), which subsequently influences social and economic development in rural areas (Shields, 2005). This line of thought stems from the view of Halfacree (2007) that rurality is a result of changing spatial practices. Spatial practices are everyday activities of rural space, which are viewed as life dimension that determines shared values and commonalities in the rural society (Halfacree, 2007). In other words, spatial practice is a set of interrelated and self-reinforcing routine activities that define rural life. Daily activities of rural residents vary depending on cultural and socio-economical contexts. Nonetheless, rural communities across the globe share certain similarities, such as the important role of social capital in supporting the viability of rural development. Shields (2005) found that rurality affects rural enterprises in differing ways: for example, manufacturing business in rural setting would be less affected by remoteness than the retail and service sectors.

Rural communities are often characterised by close social interaction (Van Dam et al., 2002) maintained via informal controls (Li et al., 2019). As highlighted in Porter's diamond model (1990), regional networks are important for creating a favourable environment for local business development. According to Henderson (2002, p. 53), 'rural communities that serve as regional economic centres have larger and more diverse economies to combat the problem of being small'. For example, the Northern Italian region Emilia-Romagna has been renowned for its complex but flexible networking between small and medium-sized firms (Cowell, 2010; Ring et al., 2010). Similarly, Gram Mooligai Company – a community-based enterprise – has had high participation rates and positive impacts in rural India (Torri, 2010).

The perception of rurality is mutually reinforced and reflected through the actions of individuals and communities as a whole. Rurality is often narrated as a *rural idyll* (Van Dam et al., 2002) and counter-urban living (Mitchell and Madden, 2014). Although rurality can be perceived in a variety of ways, its core meaning is that the rural village is associated with an idealised place of living, a utopia or a haven (Van Dam et al., 2002). In some places, rurality is marketed as a unique selling point. For example, market demand for authentic home-cooked meals may lead to the growth of food production labelled as 'rural motherhood' (Anthopoulou, 2010). The growing popularity of rural festivals is also a good example of using rurality as an attraction for tourists (Hjalager and Kwiatkowski, 2018).

One major implication of an overly positive image of rurality is that the dark side of rurality is often overlooked. For entrepreneurially minded criminals, a rural area may represent a strategic location for organised crime due to its geographical remoteness and sparsity of population (Somerville et al., 2015). Other negative attitudes towards rurality include backwardness, being monolithic, and intolerance of change (Rutten, 2001; Coldwell, 2010; Somerville et al., 2015).

To summarise, rurality may be seen as a market opportunity but also a resource constraint, depending on the eye of the beholder. An entrepreneur working in a rural setting would be in a position to turn a weakness associated with a peripheral location into a business opportunity or strength and commodify or exploit it (Anderson, 2000). This discussion of rural areas and communities shows close commonalities with deprived areas as the latter could also be associated with the dark side of rurality and characterised by increased likelihood of criminal activities and even organised crime, and by being monolithic in their values and often intolerant of change.

STUDIES OF RURAL ENTREPRENEURSHIP: SHIFTING FOCUS

Earlier studies on rural entrepreneurship often revolved around the challenges facing entrepreneurs (Cécora, 1999; Shields, 2005; Möller, 2012) and policies that have impact on rural economic development (Stathopoulou et al., 2004; North and Smallbone, 2006; Webster, 2017). Table 3.1 provides an indicative overview of research directions in the past two decades; this list is by no means exhaustive.

A closer examination of these studies indicates that the research focus has been changing over time. In the 2000s, researchers of entrepreneurship were more concerned with the resource constraints faced by rural entrepreneurs and strategic approaches taken by them to overcome those challenges. In the past, rurality was seen as adverse to the marketability of products and services (Shields, 2005). However, over the last decade the world underwent a series of social and economic changes, which is reflected in the shift of emphasis: rurality is now viewed as a more socially diverse phenomenon than before. The rise and fall of social networking sites, the counter-urban living movement, and growing numbers of digital natives, all contribute to behavioural changes in rural areas. In particular, demands for counter-urbanisation (Mitchell and Madden, 2014) and authenticity (Anthopoulou, 2010; Möller, 2012; Kordel, 2016) are on the rise, which presents market potential to rural entrepreneurs. The changing pattern of

Table 3.1. Studies in Rural Entrepreneurship (1999–2019).

Authors	Methods	Sample Size	Country under the Study	Findings
Eckert (1999)	Analysis of secondary data; case study	2	Cameroon	Two cases from colonial Cameroon represent two different trajectories in African entrepreneurship
Anderson (2000)	Interview; site visit; observation	54	Scotland	Entrepreneurs turn peripheral weakness into strength
Rutten (2001)	Case study	246	India, Malaysia, Indonesia	It is the flexibility of entrepreneurs to adjust to changing social and economic circumstances that explains the success and failure of any enterprise
Ma (2002)	Survey	2,180	China	Mobilisation of social capital is an important aspect of rural entrepreneurship in China
Smart (2003)	Interview; focus group; site visit	14	Canada	Chinese restaurant operators in rural Canada rely on socially mediated networks arising from successive transborder migrations across and between national and provincial boundaries

Table 3.1. *(Continued)*

Authors	**Methods**	**Sample Size**	**Country under the Study**	**Findings**
Frazier and Niehm (2004)	Interview	24	United States	Rural entrepreneurs engage in a variety of informal social network
Wang and Fan (2006)	Interview; survey	305; 5,484	China	The authors highlighted the prevalence of failure returnees and raised questions about the extent to which return migrants can contribute to the economic development of their places of origin
Shields (2005)	Survey	76	United States	Rural geo-demography adversely affects the marketability of products and services
Kalantaridis and Bika (2006)	Survey	100	United Kingdom	In-migrant entrepreneurs exhibit a low degree of local embeddedness, which enables them to break out of the confines of rurality
Stone and Stubbs (2007)	Interview	58	Spain and France	The interaction between migrant characteristics and local conditions produces distinctive regional patterns of rural entrepreneurship

D'haese et al. (2008)	Survey	1,001	Nicaragua	Household resources and entrepreneurial experience are significant determinants for rural businesses in all sectors
Anthopoulou (2010)	Survey	74	Greece	Rural motherhood contributes to marketability of food production
Torri (2010)	Case study; interview	32	India	Community-based enterprises see communal values as an essential element in venture creation
Möller (2012)	Case study; interview	11	Latvia	The limited growth for women's entrepreneurship is rooted in more traditionally gendered ideals of work and livelihood
Yu et al. (2013)	Content analysis of published stories	91	China	Rural entrepreneurs in China rely on social relations in dealing with constraints from the institutional environment
Mitchell and Madden (2014)	Interview	7	Canada	In-migrants contribute to commercial counter-urbanisation and serve the need of local community rather than capitalising heritage assets

Table 3.1. *(Continued)*

Authors	Methods	Sample Size	Country under the Study	Findings
Somerville et al. (2015)	Case study	5	United Kingdom	Illicit rural entrepreneurship hides behind the cloak of the rural idyll
Kordel (2016)	Interview	41	Germany	Entrepreneurs commodify rurality through combining traditional building material with luxury and intimacy elements
Webster (2017)	Interview; observation	26	Sweden	Rural context and social networks shape translocal activities
Hjalager and Kwiatkowski (2018)	Survey	315	Denmark	Business opportunities are ubiquitous in rural festivals in Denmark
Joslyn (2018)	Survey; interview	16	United States	Rural entrepreneurship is influenced by the institutional environment from which the entrepreneur originates
Zhu et al. (2019)	Interview	27	China	Rural migrant entrepreneurs receive institutional support from both host region and home town

research focus reflects the technological and lifestyle changes that affect deprived communities as well.

ENTREPRENEURIAL ORIGIN

There is a distinction between rich and poor entrepreneurs in the context of skills and financial resources. Joslyn (2018) examined the entrepreneurial differences between in-migrants coming from industrialised vs developing countries. Having studied a small sample of 16 entrepreneurs in a rural town in the United States, Joslyn (2018) reported that immigrants from developing countries face greater constraints than immigrants from developed countries in terms of mobilising start-up capital and business acumen. However, entrepreneurial origin seems to have lesser implications in the digital age since many ventures are 'born global' (Hjalager and Kwiatkowski, 2018), that is they rely heavily on technology.

In rural England, Kalantaridis and Bika (2006) found that the main difference between locally born and in-migrant entrepreneurs lies in the way both groups obtain and use insights into the local market. Based on analysis of a sample of 100 respondents, Kalantaridis and Bika (2006) reported that locally born entrepreneurs tend to rely more on local sources of information regarding market opportunities than in-migrant entrepreneurs, whereas for in-migrants engagement with the locals and acquiring local market information appears to be insignificant or even irrelevant.

In contrast, other studies, such as those by Frazier and Niehm (2004) and Stone and Stubbs (2007), emphasise the importance of establishing social networks with the local population. The ability to network with and market to the indigenous population has implications for business growth (Stone and Stubbs, 2007). In their study of lifestyle migration to rural France and Spain, they found that language skills were a defining factor for migrants in promoting their business and/or connecting with locals synergistically. Immigrants who do not speak the local language limit their business networks to expatriates and foreigners, thereby limiting business growth. This finding is consistent with the study of Smart (2003), which concluded that successful immigrants strategically navigated their way through business experience and employment in order to gain necessary know-how (including local language skills) and social capital that are instrumental for new venture creation.

Based on historical data and anthropological research, Eckert (1999) analysed rural entrepreneurship in Cameroon between the 1880s and 1950s. This study found that specific social and cultural systems jointly determined economic success in the colonial period. Despite differences in social status and traditions, two ethnic groups, Duala and Bamileke, exhibited entrepreneurial aptitude and became market leaders for decades.

RURAL–URBAN MIGRATION AND RETURN MIGRATION

In a study of returnee entrepreneurship in rural China, Ma (2002) argued that returnees represent a brain-drain reversal and highlighted the impactful role of these returnees in promoting entrepreneurial activities in their hometowns and rural communities in general. After accumulating sufficient social capital and knowledge, these migrants go back to their rural hometowns and start new businesses thereby contributing to regional growth. However, this view of returnees is incomplete: in reality, most returnees experienced failure in their entrepreneurial endeavours in rural China due to the institutional environment and social factors (Wang and Fan, 2006). First, the socialist control apparatus, namely the *hukou* system (household registration), constrains rural–urban migration in order to avoid overpopulation in the already large cities. This tight state control partially contributes to return migration as returnees often have difficulty gaining permanent residency in urban areas. Second, rural migrants are disadvantaged in the city due to labour market segmentation and institutional barriers against social and economic mobility. Many cities limit the availability of jobs to local residents thereby restricting job opportunities for rural migrants; as a result, many migrants from rural areas work in low-skilled occupations. Third, migrants may choose to return to their rural homes because of family duties rather than in search of entrepreneurial opportunity.

In a study of rural migrants in China, Zhu et al. (2019) found that entrepreneurs who moved from rural areas helped to promote economic growth and create job opportunities in both host region and home town. These rural migrants tend to employ people who come from the same home town due to kinship and township relationships. Recognising the economic implications of rural migrant entrepreneurs, the governments of both localities claim that they intend to help rural migrants to run their businesses in the host regions. However, only a small number of entrepreneurs managed to actually receive institutional support from the government (Zhu et al., 2019).

VARYING EXPERIENCE IN TRANSITIONAL ECONOMIES

The experience of rural entrepreneurship varies across the globe. In transitional (e.g. post-Soviet) economies, rural entrepreneurs may even exhibit practice that could be considered 'illicit' or perhaps 'illegal' in other countries (Somerville et al., 2015), for example tax avoidance (Möller, 2012) and bribery (Yu et al., 2013). Keeping in mind that lack of full compliance with the legal requirements is often observed in deprived areas, the practice of rural entrepreneurs aligns them even closer with entrepreneurs operating in deprived communities.

The study of Möller (2012) sheds some light on a gender aspect of entrepreneurship practice in rural Latvia during the post-Soviet period. After gaining independence from the Soviet Union, many Latvians, particularly women, lost their jobs and established their own ventures in order to break out of unemployment. Creating a new venture in the tourism industry appeared to be a good source of income with relatively low market barriers. However, these entrepreneurs encountered pressure from the lack of sufficient financial resources and the necessary know-how for running a tourism-centred or hospitality business.

Another transitional economy – China – is undergoing a series of political and socio-economic changes. The country is actively pursuing economic reforms under tight government control. Governmental support for entrepreneurs in rural areas is available for business expansion (Zhu et al., 2019). However, researchers noted that entrepreneurs rarely seek government support (Yu et al., 2013). Based on 91 published real-life stories of rural entrepreneurship in China, Yu et al. (2013) found that rural Chinese entrepreneurs rely on personal connections and rarely consider government support when creating a new venture. This may be owing to an intent to avoid excessive government control over the launch of new business ventures. Furthermore, this might be a reflection of power structures in China and related inequalities, based on the premise that lower ranking individuals in a society accept and expect that power is distributed unequally.

REGIONAL AND TRANSLOCAL NETWORKS OF RURAL ENTREPRENEURS

Business networking facilitates dissemination and exchange of information, as well as creating social connectedness between local business partners. Establishing a social network is also important for rural entrepreneurs (Ma, 2002; Frazier and Niehm, 2004; Shields, 2005; Yu et al., 2013). Recently business networking has been increasingly influenced by the notion of translocality, or translocalism, in assisting better understanding of social mobility (Webster, 2017) and interactions between local groups (Van de Poele, 2015). In other words, the metamorphosis of business networking and translocality contribute to entrepreneurial preparedness for collective action with other groups of entrepreneurs towards achieving a common goal (Van de Poele, 2015).

In China, for instance, access to valuable market information about potential business opportunities is often restricted to the key members or core of the inner circle of social networks, even though the information may be of little or no use to these insiders (Ma, 2002). Establishing personal relations (aka *guanxi*) with key representatives or insiders provides access to such information. *Guanxi* initially revolves around close friends and families as a core and then spreads outward through network ties, through exchanging personal favours over a long period of time (Yu et al., 2013). However, Zhu et al. (2019) recently reported that rural migrants in China are reluctant to expand their inner circle to avoid impairing close relationships as their businesses grow. Although many entrepreneurs are quite flexible in taking advantage of relationships with their friends or relatives during the start-up phase, they are rather cautious regarding maintaining such relationships over time in order to avoid conflict (Zhu et al., 2019).

This rather collectivistic form of entrepreneurial relationships is quite distinctive of Chinese business culture in certain Asian countries, where Chinese family businesses establish and maintain strong network ties with other family businesses (Rutten, 2001) that in many cases may be categorised as competitors in the Western tradition. The same trend can be observed outside China. For example, most Chinese restaurants in rural Canada are family owned and managed. According to Smart (2003), nearly every Canadian rural town has at least one restaurant run by a Chinese family, and these Chinese restaurant operators maintain good relationships with each other and make a conscious effort to develop active connections with their local community.

FAMILY INVOLVEMENT

Most rural enterprises involve spouses or a husband-and-wife team working together with other family members (Möller, 2012), which bears some resemblance with lifestyle entrepreneurship. Family engagement in rural entrepreneurship varies in terms of scope, i.e. it can include all activities of daily operations (Stone and Stubbs, 2007) or could be limited to financial support only (Yu et al., 2013). However, similar to the launch of other small businesses, rural entrepreneurs often rely on family labour during the start-up phase (Smart, 2003).

The Chinese family business culture is grounded in a strong sense of family and clan solidarity (Rutten, 2001). Owing to the family structure and inheritance practices, many Chinese businesses tend to accumulate considerable social capital over the years. *Guanxi* has a strong impact on the scope and depth of Chinese family enterprises (Rutten, 2001). With embedded reciprocity and mutual obligations, *guanxi* reshapes the Western concept of networking by emphasising the need to maintain long-term business and interpersonal relations with expectations of exchanging favours (Yu et al., 2013). However, it is worth noting that Chinese entrepreneurs tend to overemphasise the use of *guanxi* in traditional business and networks, whereas Chinese trading networks in contemporary settings seem to be evolving by becoming less dependent on the co-ethnic connections when integrating into the local communities. For instance, in the case of Chinese restaurant operators in rural Canada, this development reached the level of adoption of local community values and significant dissociation with ethnic values. The ultimate result was that rural Chinese restaurant operators expressed an intention not to pass on their family business to their children. This trend is in sync with value diffusion processes that are typical for deprived communities, where norms and values are often socially moderated or imposed on newcomers.

ILLICIT RURAL ENTREPRENEURSHIP

The entrepreneur is often portrayed as an innovator (Hébert and Link, 2006), a change agent (Anderson, 2000) or a self-employed person (Stone and Stubbs, 2007). Entrepreneurial activities include all sorts of actions exhibited by enterprising individuals directed towards value creation that can subsequently be exchanged via a particular medium, e.g. money or other perks. Arguably, illegal or illicit activities fit into the description of entrepreneurial activities as they may create a certain value and be sought after. The absence of a universally accepted definition of entrepreneurial activities does not exclude actions which are strictly legal and yet harmful to the environment, animals and/or societal welfare. Researchers refer to such activities, associated with entrepreneurship, as illicit or informal (Williams, 2014; Somerville et al., 2015).

The latter description could be applied to an entrepreneur who may engage in transactions not declared for tax or benefit purposes, but which are legitimate in all other aspects. The rural deprived area setting may represent a suitable context for such kind of activities owing, at least in part, to the difficulties in organising appropriate control mechanisms.

CONCEPTUALISING THE TYPOLOGY OF RURAL ENTREPRENEURSHIP IN DEPRIVED AREAS

The preceding discussion allows for the formulation of a conceptual framework summarising the identified characteristics of rural entrepreneurship applicable to entrepreneurial activities in deprived communities (Fig. 3.1). Each type of entrepreneur has varying degrees of connectedness and rurality, determined by the essence of their entrepreneurial activities. These activities can take any form across different industry sectors, ranging from artisan ventures to community-centred enterprises (Torri, 2010), having regulated or unregulated activities (Somerville et al., 2015). Largely

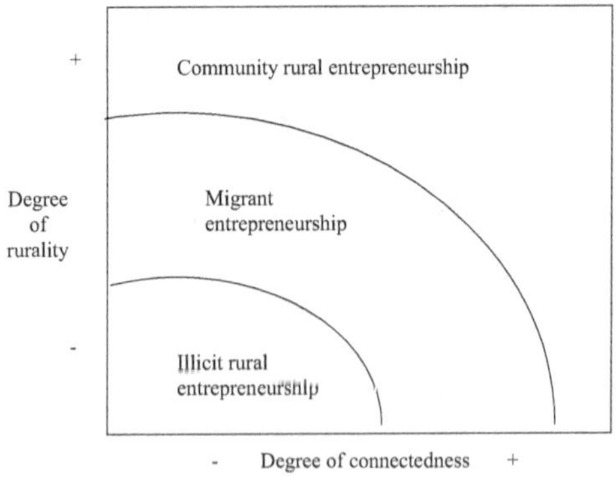

Fig. 3.1. Typology of Rural Entrepreneurship in Deprived Settings.

characterised by social capital gained in the community, rural entrepreneurs are relationship-oriented and aim to capitalise on a variety of social relations, ranging from local to transnational networks (Smart, 2003), formal association membership (Zhu et al., 2019) and informal social ties.

At one end of the spectrum, rural entrepreneurs take advantage of multiple connections and intense networking in their value creating activities. For instance, Gram Mooligai Company Limited (GMCL), a company owned by working women from several rural villages in India, is an illustrative case of rural community entrepreneurship. Traditionally, cultivating and collecting plants is the responsibility of females in India. GMCL not only employs women who live in rural areas for the purpose of collecting and processing herbs but also shares dividends with them. These women are major shareholders of GMCL, and they have opportunity to participate in the decision-making at the corporate level (Torri, 2010).

Other examples of community entrepreneurship include community enterprises, such as Tobermory Harbour Association (2018), a community-owned hub port in the Isle of Mull (a remote Scottish island). As a community non-for-profit venture, Tobermory Harbour Association manages and maintains facilities within the harbour. It has clear lines of responsibility and accountability to ensure that the harbour can continue to trade profitably and grow for the benefit of the island community. Community enterprises like Tobermory Harbour Association are not uncommon in rural areas of the United Kingdom, especially in underserved communities. They also often enjoy various degrees of government support. The UK government, for example, relaxed legal requirements, making it easier for a community to raise money to develop community-owned enterprises. Furthermore, people who do not live locally can invest in community enterprises by buying shares or providing loan stock (Birch, 2013). Similar to the

United Kingdom, in 2011 the US government introduced the Entrepreneur Access to Capital Act (H.R. 2930), which permits crowdfunding method that offers an equity stake (securities) to investors. Such law-easing interventions allow people to live away from the rural places but invest in community-owned enterprises. A community-owned rural enterprise may be viewed as a preferred form of entrepreneurship owing to its high level of connectedness that permits to combine social capital stemming from various sources. It also has a high level of rurality because it aims to promote rural development for the benefit of rural communities.

At the other end of the spectrum is the least represented form – illicit rural entrepreneurship. For informal entrepreneurs, rurality is particularly attractive because of geographical remoteness and the lower chance of getting exposed to relevant authorities. Rather than being just an extension of urban crimes, rural crimes are distinctively rural (Somerville et al., 2015). Unlike community-centred rural entrepreneurship, illicit rural entrepreneurship represents a darker side of rurality and a lower level of connectedness due to its isolated nature. The majority of informal entrepreneurial endeavours start with close social relations or rapport on a relatively small scale (Williams, 2014). Such restricted market entry implies that only the individuals in the inner circle of close associates and friends with whom the entrepreneur had/has long-term relationships can utilise the informally created value.

In rural entrepreneurship, the most represented group are migrants of the following types: immigrants, urban–rural migrants and returnees. Entrepreneurs in this group tend to mobilise resources they have accumulated over the years and to pursue entrepreneurial endeavours in rural places. Rurality for them could mean resource constraint, market opportunity or both. Webster (2017) introduces a case of rural-to-rural network (aka trans-local network) where women from rural

Thailand do business in rural Sweden. Such a rural-to-rural case is rare, although it demonstrates how immigrants make use of networks at different levels: transnational, co-ethnic and local. In a similar vein, Smart (2003, p. 337) reported that Chinese immigrants strategically and skilfully make the most of 'local social networks of co-ethnic and non-ethnic nature' that are instrumental for their entrepreneurial endeavours. Rural migrants, on the other hand, launch their products or services in urban cities (Zhu et al., 2019), and some of them even duplicate their success when they return to their home town or home country.

CONCLUSION

Entrepreneurial activities in rural areas are crucial to both local economy and regional development. Rural entrepreneurship is characterised by the notion of rurality. The meaning associated with rurality is socially constructed and for some rurality represents rural idyll (Van Dam et al., 2002; Halfacree, 2007), whereas for others rurality symbolises backwardness or underdeveloped potential (Rutten, 2001; Coldwell, 2010; Somerville et al., 2015). The studies of illicit rural entrepreneurship challenge the established view of rurality as rural idyll and shed some light on its dark side.

Rural entrepreneurship used to be characterised by enterprise in the areas with low density of population, small market size and limited supply of human resources. The increasingly digitised global economy presents alternative means for rural entrepreneurs to interact with a wider market as technology provides certain advantages for launching products or offering services through online platforms. Furthermore, engaging with other entrepreneurs in different locations can provide additional support and resources that rural enterprises may need.

Migration has been found to stimulate entrepreneurial activities in developed countries as well as in transitional economies. On one hand, in-migration provides fresh blood to the rural community and introduces different ways of doing business. On the other hand, returnees bring knowledge, capital and networks, which promote entrepreneurial activities in rural communities. The combination of migrant and returning entrepreneurs may help to rejuvenate the economy in rural and deprived areas. To summarise, spatial mobility and the openness of rural communities to new entrepreneurial thinking are important for new business creation in rural settings that often experience deprivation.

Rural entrepreneurship bears a strong resemblance to necessity entrepreneurship because rural areas have commonalities with deprived areas: they both feature low-income population, limited employment opportunities, higher crime rates and a need for revitalisation. This similarity allows transposition of the enterprise culture model associated with necessity entrepreneurship to rural context. However, the factors stimulating entrepreneurial activities in rural communities are limited principally to two areas: (1) there are possibilities for significantly more extensive use of information technology to overcome the rurality's constraints and (2) opportunities to increase government support in the form of effective policies and wider availability of grants. The factors hindering rural entrepreneurship in deprived areas can be summarised as the lack of training and overall preparedness to launch and subsequently manage the venture, overconfidence in the capacity to manage a business and estimate risks, and lack of understanding of market opportunities. Altogether, developments in rural entrepreneurship, particularly associated with the role of government in stimulating rural enterprising, appear promising in turning the tide and give hope to the next generation of rural entrepreneurs and their respective communities.

LEARNING POINTS

- Collectivistic forms of relationships (e.g. via family or ethnic ties) are common in rural enterprises, particularly in Asian economies. Local governing bodies might be able to further strengthen these forms by offering incentives to collective community business ventures.
- A community-owned rural enterprise offers a high degree of connectedness with the local residents and their needs and, hence, shows stability as it is able to mobilise all kinds of social capital.
- Special attention needs to be paid to promoting market opportunities in rural areas, e.g. by local newsletters, events and sharing best practice.
- Novel methods of investment (e.g. crowdfunding via selling shares) allow people who live away from rural areas to invest in community-owned enterprises. These methods should be promoted to both rural and urban population, highlighting newly available opportunities to potential investors.

REFERENCES

Anderson, A.R. 2000. Paradox in the periphery: an entrepreneurial reconstruction? *Entrepreneurship & Regional Development*, 12(2), 91–109.

Anthopoulou, T. 2010. Rural women in local agrofood production: between entrepreneurial initiatives and family strategies. A case study in Greece. *Journal of Rural Studies*, 26(4), 394–403.

Birch, S. 2013. Community ownership popularity rising. *The Guardian*, 12 February. Available at: https://www.theguardian.com/social-enterprise-network/2013/feb/12/community-ownership-enjoys-surge-popularity

Coldwell, I. 2010. Retracted: masculinities in the rural and the agricultural: a literature review. *Sociologia Ruralis*, 50(2), 171–197.

Cowell, M. 2010. Polycentric regions: comparing complementarity and institutional governance in the San Francisco Bay Area, the Randstad and Emilia-Romagna. *Urban Studies*, 47(5), 945–965.

Cécora, J. 1999. *Cultivating Grass-Roots for Regional Development in a Globalising Economy*, Aldershot, Ashgate.

D'haese, M., De Ruijter De Wildt, M. and Ruben, R. 2008. Business incomes in rural Nicaragua: the role of household resources, location, experience and trust. *Entrepreneurship & Regional Development*, 20(4), 345–366.

Eckert, A. 1999. African rural entrepreneurs and labor in the Cameroon littoral. *The Journal of African History*, 40(1), 109–126.

Frazier, B.J. and Niehm, L.S. 2004. Exploring business information networks of small retailers in rural communities. *Journal of Developmental Entrepreneurship*, 9(1), 23–42.

Halfacree, K. 2007. Trial by space for a 'radical rural': introducing alternative localities, representations and lives. *Journal of Rural Studies*, 23(2), 125–141.

Hébert, R.F. and Link, A.N. 2006. The entrepreneur as innovator. *The Journal of Technology Transfer*, 31(5), 589–597.

Henderson, J. 2002. Building the rural economy with high-growth entrepreneurs. *Federal Reserve Bank of Kansas City Economic Review*, 87(3), 45–70.

Hjalager, A. and Kwiatkowski, G. 2018. Entrepreneurial implications, prospects and dilemmas in rural festivals. *Journal of Rural Studies*, 63, 217–228.

Hoggart, K. 1990. Let's do away with rural. *Journal of Rural Studies*, 6(3), 245–257.

Joslyn, J. 2018. A comparison of sources of business acumen for entrepreneurs originating from developed and developing countries. *Journal of Rural Social Sciences*, 33(1), 101–114.

Kalantaridis, C. and Bika, Z. 2006. In-migrant entrepreneurship in rural England: beyond local embeddedness. *Entrepreneurship & Regional Development*, 18(2), 109–131.

Kordel, S. 2016. Selling ruralities: how tourist entrepreneurs commodify traditional and alternative ways of conceiving the countryside. *Rural Society*, 25(3), 204–221.

Korsgaard, S., Müller, S. and Tanvig, H. 2015. Rural entrepreneurship or entrepreneurship in the rural – between place and space. *International Journal of Entrepreneurial Behavior & Research*, 21(1), 5–26.

Li, Y., Westlund, H. and Liu, Y. 2019. Why some rural areas decline while some others not: an overview of rural evolution in the world. *Journal of Rural Studies*, 68, 135–143.

Ma, Z. 2002. Social-capital mobilization and income returns to entrepreneurship: the case of return migration in rural China. *Environment and Planning A*, 34(10), 1763–1784.

Möller, C. 2012. Gendered entrepreneurship in rural Latvia: exploring femininities, work, and livelihood within rural tourism. *Journal of Baltic Studies*, 43(1), 75–94.

Mitchell, C. and Madden, M. 2014. Re-thinking commercial counterurbanisation: evidence from rural Nova Scotia, Canada. *Journal of Rural Studies*, 36, 137–148.

North, D. and Smallbone, D. 2006. Developing entrepreneurship and enterprise in Europe's peripheral rural areas: some issues facing policy-makers. *European Planning Studies*, 14(1), 41–60.

Porter, M. 1990. The competitive advantage of nations. *Harvard Business Review*, 68(2), 73–93.

Ring, J.K., Peredo, A.M. and Chrisman, J.J. 2010. Business networks and economic development in rural communities in the United States. *Entrepreneurship: Theory and Practice*, 34(1), 171–195.

Rutten, M. 2001. Family enterprises and business partnerships: rural entrepreneurs in India, Malaysia, and Indonesia. *Journal of Entrepreneurship*, 10(2), 165–189.

Shields, J.F. 2005. Does rural location matter? The significance of a rural setting for small businesses. *Journal of Developmental Entrepreneurship*, 10(1), 49–63.

Smart, J. 2003. Ethnic entrepreneurship, transmigration, and social integration: an ethnographic study of Chinese restaurant owners in rural Western Canada. *Urban Anthropology and Studies of Cultural Systems and World Economic Development*, 32(3/4), 311–342.

Somerville, P., Smith, R. and McElwee, G. 2015. The dark side of the rural idyll: stories of illegal/illicit economic activity in the UK countryside. *Journal of Rural Studies*, 39, 219–228.

Stathopoulou, S., Psaltopoulos, D. and Skuras, D. 2004. Rural entrepreneurship in Europe: a research framework and agenda. *International Journal of Entrepreneurial Behaviour & Research*, 10(6), 404–425.

Stone, I. and Stubbs, C. 2007. Enterprising expatriates: lifestyle migration and entrepreneurship in rural southern Europe. *Entrepreneurship & Regional Development*, 19(5), 433–450.

Tobermory Harbour Association. 2018. *Company Management*. Available at: https://www.tobermoryharbour.co.uk/company-management

Torri, M. 2010. Community-based enterprises: a promising basis towards an alternative entrepreneurial model for sustainability enhancing livelihoods and promoting socio-economic development in rural India. *Journal of Small Business and Entrepreneurship*, 23(2), 237–248.

Van Dam, F., Heins, S. and Elbersen, B.S. 2002. Lay discourses of the rural and stated and revealed preferences for rural living. Some evidence of the existence of a rural idyll in the Netherlands. *Journal of Rural Studies*, 18(4), 461–476.

Van de Poele, L. 2015. Rural development from the grassroots: twenty years of the EU "Leader approach". In *Constructing a New Framework for Rural Development (Research in Rural Sociology and Development)*, Eds P. Milone, F. Ventura and J. Ye, Vol. 22, pp. 195–207, Bingley, Emerald Publishing Limited.

Wang, W. and Fan, C. 2006. Success or failure: selectivity and reasons of return migration in Sichuan and Anhui, China. *Environment and Planning: A*, 38(5), 939–958.

Webster, N.A. 2017. Rural-to-rural translocal practices: Thai women entrepreneurs in the Swedish countryside. *Journal of Rural Studies*, 56, 219–228.

Williams, C.C. 2014. *Informal Sector Entrepreneurship*. OECD Policy Briefing Background Paper. Paris, OECD.

Yu, J., Zhou, J.X., Wang, Y. and Xi, Y. 2013. Rural entrepreneurship in an emerging economy: reading institutional perspectives from entrepreneur stories. *Journal of Small Business Management*, 51(2), 183–195.

Zhu, H., Feng, J. and Pan, F. 2019. Mixed embeddedness and entrepreneurial activities of rural migrants in the host region: the case of Yuhuan City, China. *Journal of Urban Affairs*, 41(3), 390–404.

4

SENIOR ENTREPRENEURSHIP: AGEING, ENTREPRENEURIAL IDENTITY, BEHAVIOUR AND CHALLENGES

INTRODUCTION

Interest in senior entrepreneurship is on the rise, owing to the social and economic changes related to the ageing population in many countries across the globe. Individuals associated with this type of entrepreneurship may establish their ventures in deprived areas or reside there. The potential for a positive impact on deprived communities, arising from activities of senior entrepreneurs, is the focus of this chapter.

With many baby boomers reaching retirement age, the age dependency ratio has gradually been increasing. This implies that the working population is likely to be subject to increased taxes to compensate for a larger number of individuals of dependent age (i.e. retirees and children) as the non-working populace grows. While advances in medical science and healthcare ensure longer and increasing life expectancy, the burden on the working population is on the rise, too.

Discussion of extending the working life of the ageing population to reduce the level of dependence on welfare benefits and pensions has been ongoing over many years, with countries, such as Malaysia and Indonesia, increasing the retirement age from 55 to 60 and 56 to 65, respectively. However, retaining older workers and retirees in employment is not without certain problems, such as age discrimination (Franck, 2010; Ainsworth and Hardy, 2013; Kibler et al., 2015; OECD, 2015; Stirzaker and Galloway, 2017), work experience that is either out-of-date (Kenny and Rossiter, 2018) or too narrow (Baucus and Human, 1994).

From the societal perspective, promoting senior entrepreneurship may help alleviate growing age dependency pressures and labour shortages. Helping people reaching retirement age or during their retirement years to remain economically active is the task for many communities, both deprived and successful, as seniors' contribution to society, at all levels, may be significant. It is therefore not surprising that research and policy discussions have turned their attention to senior entrepreneurship, often associated with establishing a new venture while being over retirement age.

WHO ARE SENIOR ENTREPRENEURS?

Statistics show that the number of start-ups created by individuals over 50 is smaller than the number launched by the younger generations. In an attempt to rationalise this fact, Lévesque and Minniti (2006) argue that entrepreneurial activity declines with age due to the individual's perception that the working time necessary for entrepreneurship is much greater and less fruitful than the time needed for waged labour. Hence, as experience and waged labour's rewards increase over time, the willingness of individuals to invest their time in starting a new venture diminishes. Similarly, Skirbekk (2008) argues that job performance and productivity decrease with age due to unavoidable age-related reductions in cognitive abilities.

Despite certain age limitations to senior entrepreneurship, there are many success stories of retirees who started a new business during their retirement years. Andrew Carnegie was in his late 50s when he formed the Carnegie Steel Company, and Colonel Sanders was in his 60s when he launched Kentucky Fried Chicken. Having established and developed their empires, Andrew Carnegie and Colonel Sanders remained active even after they sold their companies.

In contrast to Lévesque and Minniti (2006), Botham and Graves (2009) suggest that the probability of creating a new venture and ensuring its growth and survival increases with age, before reaching the retirement age. This difference in opinions regarding the ability and likelihood of pre-retirement individuals to engage in entrepreneurial activity most likely appeared owing to the focus of many researchers and policymakers on the biological age, rather than any other perspective on ageing. Iparraguirre (2018) asserts that, in addition to the process of biological ageing, two other aspects of ageing have to be considered in the assessment of the capabilities of individuals: psychological ageing and social ageing. Furthermore, each of these aspects is rather heterogeneous combining a variable number of other conceptualisations of age: cognitive, self-perceived, subjective and ideal.

Nonetheless, categorisation by biological age prevails. Global Entrepreneurship Monitor, an organisation conducting annual assessments of entrepreneurial activity in the countries across the globe, prepared a special report entitled *GEM Special Report on Senior Entrepreneurship 2017*, categorising entrepreneurs into four age groups: young

(18–29), mid-age (30–49), senior (50–64) and older (65–80) (Fig. 4.1). Data for 2016 show that in the Middle East and North Africa the percentage of older entrepreneurs (9%) is higher than senior entrepreneurs (7%) (Schøtt et al., 2017). Other world regions exhibit a relationship between business creation and age profile, which may be viewed as typical: out of the total adult population, mid-aged group gives the largest percentage of entrepreneurs, followed by a smaller percentage of young entrepreneurs. For example, in Latin America and the Caribbean, mid-aged group (21%) and young entrepreneurs (18%) give the total of 39% of all entrepreneurs (Schøtt et al., 2017). Seniors come next (14%), followed by even smaller percentage of entrepreneurs in the older age group (6%) (Schøtt et al., 2017). The similar, age-related, pattern of business formation is observed in other regions across the globe.

The above-noted pattern of business formation has been historically associated with perceptions of ageing as a

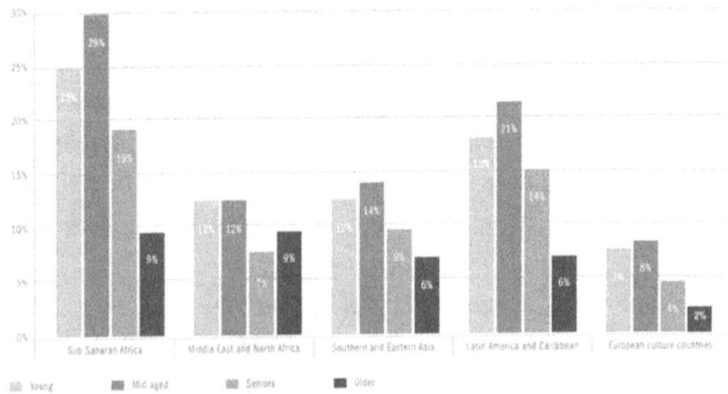

Source: Schøtt et al. (2017, p. 38).

Fig. 4.1. Early-stage Entrepreneurial Activity (as % of the Adult Population), by Age and Region, GEM 2009–2016.

biological process characterised by a weakening of the cognitive abilities of the elderly negatively affecting entrepreneurial activity (Skirbekk, 2008; Botham and Graves, 2009) and causing a decline in entrepreneurial intentions (Verheul and Van Mil, 2011; Sahut et al., 2015). Verheul and Van Mil (2011) also found that ambition for growth is negatively affected by entrepreneurs' age. The authors argue that having greater experience may dampen the ambition of senior entrepreneurs, compared to their younger counterparts, as seniors may value future financial earnings less.

In addition to start-ups that show a distinct pattern of business formation related to certain age groups, there is a large number of long-established ventures by founders who now have reached the retirement age. This poses the core question: Who should be considered a senior entrepreneur?

There has been a lack of consensus in describing this group of entrepreneurs or determining the exact age group to be referred to as senior entrepreneurs. In their study of senior entrepreneurs in Portugal, Figueiredo and Paiva (2019) examined entrepreneurs between the ages of 45 and 60, whereas Singh (2009, p. 48) referred to older entrepreneurs as 'individuals aged 55 and older' in studying generational differences between young and older entrepreneurs in America. Weber and Schaper (2004, p. 152) suggested that retirement age is the 'rightful cut-off point'; however, retirement age varies widely, which adds complexity to data collection and conceptual categorisation. In Indonesia, retirement age is currently set at 57 years old, in Iceland it is 67 and the United Kingdom recently announced plans to extend working life to 75 years of age. The differences in an official, stated in the laws, retirement age also reflect differences in life expectancy in countries across the world.

In addition to disagreement about the exact age group of senior entrepreneurs, researchers also refer to seniors differently. The most widely adopted terms are:

- *senior entrepreneurship* (Schøtt et al., 2017; Perenyi et al., 2018; Figueiredo and Paiva, 2019);
- *older entrepreneurship* (Singh, 2009; Stirzaker and Galloway, 2017; Ratten, 2019);
- *third age entrepreneurship* (Botham and Graves, 2009; Lewis and Walker, 2013);
- *grey entrepreneurship* (Weber and Schaper, 2004; Watkins-Mathys, 2012);
- *second career entrepreneurship* (Baucus and Human, 1994); and
- *encore entrepreneurship* (Jurinski et al., 2016).

Irrespective of the differences in age grouping and terminology, these terms generally refer to older entrepreneurs as someone who creates a new business at a later stage in their life (Baucus and Human, 1994; Weber and Schaper, 2004; Botham and Graves, 2009; Singh, 2009; Jurinski et al., 2016; Figueiredo and Paiva, 2019). Table 4.1 summarises these differences in describing senior entrepreneurs.

Additionally, defining senior entrepreneurship based on the age of the founder and emphasising seniors' role in new venture creation excludes those entrepreneurs who have built successful business before reaching their 50s and who have continued to engage in entrepreneurial activities beyond the officially stated retirement age. Iconic examples of such entrepreneurs are Richard Branson with his Virgin Group and Bill Gates with the Bill & Melinda Gates Foundation.

These entrepreneurs, notwithstanding their age and wealth, actively continue to pursue their entrepreneurial endeavours.

Table 4.1. Summary of Differences in Categorising Senior Entrepreneurs.

Authors	Age Group	Terminology Used
Figueiredo and Paiva (2019)	45–60	Senior entrepreneurship
Perenyi et al. (2018)	50 and older	Senior entrepreneurship
Schøtt et al. (2017)	50–64	Senior entrepreneurship
Schøtt et al. (2017)	65–80	Older entrepreneurship
Kautonen et al. (2008)	50 and older	Older entrepreneurship
Stirzaker and Galloway (2017)	50 and older	Older entrepreneurship
Singh (2009)	55 and older	Older entrepreneurship
Lewis and Walker (2013)	50 and older	Third age entrepreneurship
Botham and Graves (2009)	Over 50	Third age entrepreneurship
Weber and Schaper (2004)	Over 50	Grey entrepreneurship
Watkins-Mathys (2012)	Over 50	Grey entrepreneurship
Baucus and Human (1994)	39–60	Second career entrepreneurship

AGE AND AGEING: SOCIALLY CONSTRUCTED CATEGORIES

Attempting to better comprehend senior entrepreneurship, a social constructionist perspective might allow insights into a better understanding of age and ageing. From this perspective, age and ageing are socially constructed as our cognition of the world stems from active involvement with people and their surroundings (Kautonen, 2012; Stypińska, 2018). While ageing is a biological process, the meaning of such perceptions as 'being youthful' or 'getting older' is socially constructed. Having an emphasis on socially and culturally situated knowledge, in the social constructionist view ageing is part of the individual's identity. For example, seniority is traditionally associated with wisdom and, thus, should be treated with respect. Society's perception of ageing and related expectations have an impact on the decisions made by individuals in the later part of their life. A stereotypical picture of older people as 'stagnant' or an 'encumbrance' not only pushes the elderly out of working life (Nilsson, 2016, p. 497) but also affects self-efficacy of the older people conceiving and implementing start-ups (Kautonen, 2012).

Given the dynamic nature of the social constructionist view, some authors use the expression 'subjective age', 'self-perceived age' and/or 'age identity' while referring to the social construct of age (Iparraguirre, 2018). Chronological age, by contrast, refers to 'the number of years you have lived or the distance in years since your birth' (Iparraguirre, 2018, p. 7). Researchers identified differences between chronological age and self-perceived age. For example, Franck (2010) reported that in a study of 36 women hawkers in Malaysia respondents collectively and repeatedly commented 'I am too old' as the main reason for not re-entering labour market, although they were under 50 at the time the research was conducted. Although such a sample may be too small for drawing generalisations, it highlights how individuals in the Malaysian society perceive age and ageing.

Understanding of ageing certainly is culture-bound. Crawford and Naar (2015, p. 103) found that 'feeling young and capable' is one of the reasons older Americans consider bed and breakfast as their prospective entrepreneurial venture. Schøtt et al. (2017) collected narratives of senior entrepreneurs from around the world and nearly half of them felt that age gives them certain advantages owing to a broader perspective or more informed worldview. Although such discrepancies can be explained by social and cultural differences, it also indicates an 'age-based image of entrepreneurial self' (Kautonen et al., 2015) as well as societal expectations of the role of older people.

To a large extent, social expectations regarding the role of the elderly in society do influence entrepreneurial intentions and behaviours at an older age (Weber and Schaper, 2004; Kautonen, 2012; Stypińska, 2018). Senior entrepreneurs also encounter age discrimination (Kibler et al., 2015), especially in the early stage of business formation (Botham and Graves, 2009). Social norms and stereotypes dictate age-appropriate behaviours, signposting what kinds of behaviours are deemed acceptable by social standards. For example, responsibility and expectations increase with age. It is interesting to note that older women entrepreneurs not only reject traditional social expectations towards gender but also reject the masculine-orientated entrepreneurial identity (Stirzaker and Sitko, 2019) and do not hesitate to redefine their own entrepreneurial identity (Ainsworth and Hardy, 2013).

The social aspect of age categorisation draws additional attention to the way policymakers prefer to support and/or punish according to which age-group people are in. For example, the differential treatment of adult and underage offenders is an indicator how legal institutions define criminal responsibility according to age. In the United Kingdom, for instance, children under 10 cannot be arrested or charged with a crime even if they break the law. Such predilections are also reflected in policy initiatives, where support measures for start-ups are limited to certain age groups.

Age identity is determined by self-perceived age (Iparraguirre, 2018) and 'response-ability' (Kibler et al., 2015; Stypińska, 2018) as well as by the context provided by life stage (Stirzaker and Sitko, 2019). Kautonen et al. (2015) concluded that the key to understanding age identity in respect of entrepreneurial endeavours is grounded in the perception of the individual. If a person perceives own age as favourable for entrepreneurial activities, it is likely that this individual would pursue the development of an enterprise.

Poor health and life events, such as career changes or transitions into parenthood, make people aware of their ageing and thus affect self-perceived age (Crawford and Naar, 2015). While some seniors undergo a smooth identity transition from an employee to a senior entrepreneur (Perenyi et al., 2018), others may encounter difficulties in adjusting self-identity to the status of senior entrepreneur. In exploring the entrepreneurial identity of older women entrepreneurs in the United Kingdom, Stirzaker and Sitko (2018) found that timing and life stage are important for forming entrepreneurial identity of these women. Timing and life stage also conflicted with traditional gender roles, with some experiencing difficulties in combining the role of mother and entrepreneur. Equally, in developing countries, female entrepreneurship is found to be restricted by gendered norms and practices (Franck, 2010).

Attitudes at societal and organisational levels affect the working experience and perception of older workers, which subsequently affects their decision to remain in the labour market or pursue a start-up. In a study of age-related social expectations, Kautonen (2012, p. 185) found that the 'general public's perception of the economic contribution to society made by older people is negatively associated with the entrepreneurial engagement of individuals aged 50–74 years'. This statement shows a societal bias against older workers as entrepreneurs, which may also affect the individual's assumptions regarding their own role in society in respect of entrepreneurial intentions and behaviours at an older age, effectively leading to lower rates of start-ups among older people.

Social acceptability and expectations of older entrepreneurs differ from country to country (Kautonen, 2012; Kibler et al., 2015; Stypińska, 2018) and by gender (Franck, 2010; Stirzaker and Sitko, 2019). One reason for the declining rate of entrepreneurial activity among older people is that they find it difficult to adapt to the youthful image of the entrepreneur, which is prevalent in many countries (Ainsworth and Hardy, 2013; Kibler et al., 2015). Some studies (Crawford and Naar, 2015; Kibler et al., 2015; Perenyi et al., 2018) found that a supportive spouse and positive judgements by friends and family instil confidence and motivation, and stimulate activities leading to becoming senior entrepreneurs. Perenyi et al. (2018) noted that social influences do not have a direct impact on entrepreneurial activity. Instead, they influence the perception of opportunities and intrinsic motivations. The authors argued that positive feedback from the family as well as the ability to cope with negative social feedback and social (dis-)approval may influence the intrinsic motivation for pursuing the creation of a new venture.

Equally, social influences play a significant role in assessing a person's own entrepreneurial preparedness or recovery from a failure. Kenny and Rossiter (2018, p. 248), in evaluating effectiveness of entrepreneurship training and mentoring programmes, noted that ongoing support may alleviate isolation and doubts, and encourage entrepreneurial aspiration towards new business creation. Similarly, Lin and Wang

(2019) indicate that the speed of recovery from an entrepreneurial failure is faster for older entrepreneurs as a result of their capacity to learn from failure. Furthermore, the speed of launching another venture increases with experience and strong family support.

THE LANDSCAPE OF RESEARCH ON SENIOR ENTREPRENEURSHIP

Earlier research on senior entrepreneurship revolves around barriers faced by (Kautonen et al., 2008; Kenny and Rossiter, 2018; Martin and Welsch, 2019) and motivation of (Botham and Graves, 2009; Schøtt et al., 2017; Figueiredo and Paiva, 2019) seniors. A number of studies discussed the effectiveness of policy initiatives for supporting senior entrepreneurship, such as business advisory support (Weber and Schaper, 2004), incubators (Stypińska et al., 2019), start-up or innovation grants (Botham and Graves, 2009), start-up funding (Kautonen et al., 2008), virtual networking (OECD, 2015) and educational programmes (Kenny and Rossiter, 2018).

One of the critical determinants of setting up a business by older people, which is not sufficiently captured by the extant studies, is health. The possibility of deteriorating health increases with age, making people less likely to be putting much energy into business formation (Botham and Graves, 2009). Other commonly cited barriers to senior entrepreneurship include: age bias and discrimination (Kibler et al., 2015); absence of support programmes and measures (Figueiredo and Paiva, 2019); lack of financing (Franck, 2010; Kenny and Rossiter, 2018); social acceptability (Kautonen, 2012); and low level of skills in information and communication technology (Figueiredo and Paiva, 2019) (Table 4.2).

Table 4.2. Arguments *for* and *against* Senior Entrepreneurship.

Author	Sample Size; Method	Country	Findings
Argument for, i.e. age as an advantage			
Baucus and Human (1994)	7; case study	US	Relationships exist among retirees' prior employment experience, their perceptions of departure, the types of business opportunities selected, use of networks and the type of processes used to get into business
Kautonen et al. (2008)	283; survey	UK	An individual's career history has a significant impact on the likelihood of his or her switching to self-employment at an older age
Stirzaker and Galloway (2017)	20; interview	UK	All the participants of this study had experienced the negative event of redundancy before entering entrepreneurship and the outcomes are perceived as positive and contributory to their lives
Martin and Welsch (2019)	Literature review	–	Older entrepreneurs organise their social capital that they have

Table 4.2. (*Continued*)

Author	Sample Size; Method	Country	Findings
			nurtured along their previous career, by mobilising specific resources needed at each stage of the business cycle
Argument against, i.e. age as a disadvantage			
Ainsworth and Hardy (2013)	20; public hearings	Australia	Older workers are unlikely to be successful entrepreneurs because they lack the necessary skills and fail to seek advisory support
Lévesque and Minniti (2006)	Economics study	–	Opportunity costs of embarking on the entrepreneurial journey increase with the increasing age of an individual
Gray (2007)	Literature review	UK	Although many retirees may wish to become entrepreneurs, very few have the experience and knowledge basis to do so – at least not profitably
Lin and Wang (2019)	268; survey	China	The older the serial entrepreneur, the longer it takes to start a venture again

MOTIVATION FOR START-UPS

It is never too late to reinvent yourself. The motivation driving an intention to establish a venture varies for senior entrepreneurs. Based on GEM data collected from 2009 to 2017, Schøtt et al. (2017, p. 49) summarised that 'in developed economies, the older population often feels the need to do something to keep their minds active' whereas 'in developing economies, older people often have the need to work and earn income and the only way they can do this is to start their own business'. While this conclusion is valid in its essence, it neglects the complexity associated with the dynamics of life stages, cultural influences and the competitive environment where senior entrepreneurs operate.

For example, in Portugal, skilled unemployed individuals between the ages of 45 and 60 tend to be forced into long-term unemployment and are therefore more likely to launch a small business at a later stage of their lives out of necessity (Figueiredo and Paiva, 2019). In the United Kingdom, older people can be motivated to become senior entrepreneurs by a broad range of factors including difficulties with finding a job (8%), attempting to prevent an existing business from closing (10%), developing a hobby (15%), lack of career progression (22%) and the prospect of gaining independence (24%) (Botham and Graves, 2009). In Malaysia, the start-up motivations of older women include involuntary exclusion from labour market, possibility of receiving extra income and increased flexibility and autonomy (Franck, 2010). It thus appears that various difficulties and the prospects of a better life may push older people towards entrepreneurial aspirations.

To complete an overview of the motivations for launching a new venture, governmental support needs to be mentioned. Countries that lack the capacity to provide or manage a state pension scheme are more likely to have higher levels of entrepreneurial activity in their older age populations, mostly driven by the fear of poverty (Perenyi et al., 2018).

ARGUMENTS AGAINST SENIOR ENTREPRENEURSHIP

The argument against senior entrepreneurship can be succinctly expressed by citing words of Gray (2007, p. 13) articulating that contemplating and getting involved in 'entrepreneurship for the first time after 60 is probably foolish and ill advised'.

In a study of older unemployed people in Australia, Ainsworth and Hardy (2013, p. 398) argued that 'older workers were unlikely to be successful entrepreneurs; and therefore should be discouraged from attempting it'. It is important to note that data used in this study were collected between 1999 and 2000, based on 20 public hearings regarding an Australian Parliamentary inquiry on 'the social, economic and industrial issues specific to workers over 45 years of age seeking employment, or establishing a business, following unemployment' (Ainsworth and Hardy, 2013, pp. 392–393). The study refers to older, unemployed workers as an 'unattractive product' and pursuit of entrepreneurship as a 'risky project' for older people. The authors further described this group of older unemployed people as lacking the necessary skills, failing to calculate risks and not seeking advisory support. As a result of desperation in seeking employment, people of this group tend to make 'flawed decisions' and may have bought a small business on impulse (Ainsworth and Hardy, 2013, p. 401) without concrete chances of managing it well.

More recently, Perenyi et al. (2018, p. 98) found that 'Australian senior entrepreneurs are primarily opportunity motivated, and necessity has little to do with their entrepreneurial intent'. Although this study did not indicate that Australian senior entrepreneurs are more successful than their younger counterparts, it shows a more positive image of senior entrepreneurs because they do not act out of desperation arising from unemployment. Some older women see business creation as an extra household income, secondary to their family obligations (Franck, 2010; Stirzaker and Sitko, 2019), suggesting that older women entrepreneurs are more lifestyle-oriented rather than opportunity- or necessity-driven.

The argument against senior entrepreneurship, as advanced by Ainsworth and Hardy (2013), seems to be largely dictated by an assumption of 'flawed decision-making'. However, the authors did not provide any empirical evidence supporting the claim that the decisions made by seniors are flawed or demonstrating a low survival rate of ventures established by senior entrepreneurs.

While recognising the desire to work for themselves, other arguments against senior entrepreneurship emphasise an increased opportunity cost of time with age (Lévesque and Minniti, 2006), longer recovery period after business failure (Lin and Wang, 2019) and lack of relevant experience and knowledge (Gray, 2007).

In order to evaluate the effectiveness of senior entrepreneurs their ventures can be compared to those established by their younger counterparts. In one such study in the United States, Singh (2009) observes that there were no significant differences in the reported *income levels* between younger and senior entrepreneurs. Both groups of entrepreneurs had higher income than their respective comparison groups (i.e. individuals in paid employment). However, Botham and Graves (2009) found that young entrepreneurs perform better in terms of number of employees engaged in their firms. It was also found that mixed-age teams performed even better but younger founders tend to be more growth-oriented. This finding is supported by other studies (e.g. Kenny and Rossiter, 2018) noting that senior entrepreneurs lack the desire to scale up their businesses.

SENIOR ENTREPRENEURSHIP IN DEPRIVED COMMUNITIES

There have been a very few studies examining senior entrepreneurship in deprived areas or among disadvantaged groups. According to GEM data from 2009 to 2016, certain geographical areas (sub-Saharan Africa and Southern and East Asia) show quite high rates of necessity-driven entrepreneurial activities in senior and older age groups. Schøtt et al. (2017, pp. 38–39) explain that 'in poorer communities in these regions, with high levels of competition for jobs, people over 50 are likely forced into necessity-entrepreneurship because of a lack of other options for sustainable livelihoods'. This situation indicates that the boundaries between senior and necessity entrepreneurs are getting thinner and allow to propose a new sub-category – necessity-driven senior entrepreneurship.

A closer examination of the senior entrepreneurs' motivation for start-ups in deprived communities allows to draw a rather complex picture. For example, Franck (2010) studied a range of women moving from the domain of formal employment to informal entrepreneurship with age. It was found that these women were driven by the flexibility of micro-level entrepreneurship, in addition to difficulties with finding a job and expecting better financial prospects. Although it was noted that these women did not generate substantial financial returns, they were able to gain social and spatial mobility.

Research on enterprising behaviour by socially disadvantaged older people in developed countries is limited.

Kautonen et al. (2008) examine the potential for, and barriers to, older enterprise as well as the role and contribution of specific enterprise-support policies, focusing on socially disadvantaged older people in the United Kingdom. The most interesting findings revolve around financial protection and the availability of funding. Regarding the benefits regime in the United Kingdom, it appears that the high level of financial security provided by the state has a negative impact on the willingness of older unemployed people to consider self-employment. An absence of financial support for disadvantaged groups forced them to launch their enterprises relying mainly on social networks and limited grants. The latter often provide services or support, rather than financing, e.g. innovation vouchers for the smaller businesses.

A CASE OF A SENIOR ENTREPRENEUR

Paul Tasner was made redundant at the age of 64 after working continuously for 40 years in small and large companies. He quickly realised that retirement was not an option because of his active mindset and took advantage of his good networks, reputation and solid engineering background by engaging in a consulting career. However, this did not give him any satisfaction. So, he began entertaining an idea, born from his concern for the environment, to work on replacing the toxic, disposable plastic packaging with environmentally friendly packaging. It was a concern to Paul that the environment burden would be left to future generations to resolve. This idea felt meaningful to him as it resonated with his beliefs about reducing the environmental impact caused by voluminous single-use plastic packaging dumped each year, polluting land, rivers and oceans.

After exploring a range of options for implementing his idea, he realised that the most logical choice to proceed was by building his own business. The venture would focus on designing and manufacturing biodegradable packaging from paper and agricultural, as well as textile, waste. Coming from a technical background, it was not easy for him to deal with all of the business issues that arose, such as manufacturing, outsourcing, job creation, patents, partnerships and securing funding, to name a few. One of the most challenging issues was funding as he was forced to compete with other, often much younger, very capable people from high-tech industries. Paul found that this process was psychologically discouraging and intimidating. It involved a steep learning curve, but his passion to do something meaningful in the global marketplace prevailed over all difficulties.

One of the key challenges in the after-survival stage was the growth of the company – PulpWorks. The revenues have doubled every year, a patent for a specific type of clean technology was obtained, and Paul's company has won more than 20 awards for its contribution to minimising the environmental burden of the worldwide plastic pollution. This afforded him with the most rewarding and meaningful experience in his life.

This is the journey of Paul Tasner, CEO of PulpWorks, who became an entrepreneur for the very first time at the age of 66, following the loss of his job after spending 40 years in paid employment (Tasner, 2017).

CONCLUSION

Senior entrepreneurs have diverse social and economic backgrounds. The intersection of age and entrepreneurship often appeared to discourage older people from taking part in entrepreneurial activities. Nonetheless, in many cases they were able to gain an entrepreneurial identity by redefining entrepreneurship and disconnecting it from youth. Research on senior entrepreneurship demonstrates that older people face a number of challenges in pursuing their entrepreneurial endeavours and yet, at the same time, it appears that these barriers can be overcome.

The vast majority of seniors had moved along the continuum from employment to entrepreneurship with age. Although some senior entrepreneurs have established businesses before reaching their 50s, little work has been done in exploring the experience of senior serial entrepreneurs. Some studies investigated the transition from unemployment to senior entrepreneurship and concluded that many seniors experienced entrepreneurship as silver lining (Stirzaker and Galloway, 2017), empowerment (Kenny and Rossiter, 2018) and a better option compared to employment (Franck, 2010). In contrast, Ainsworth and Hardy (2013) described the decisions made by older unemployed people to establish or buy a business as flawed.

Strong societal influences on senior entrepreneurs, e.g. in terms of triggering their intent to be useful to their communities, and their potential to have an impact on deprived areas should not be overlooked. Although it is not easy to swiftly revitalise the deprived neighbourhoods, it might be much easier for the community activists to create favourable conditions and expectations for seniors and, therefore, mobilise them to launch small businesses.

After consolidation of the identified characteristics of senior entrepreneurship into a model of enterprise culture in deprived communities, the following insights could be drawn. The factors stimulating entrepreneurial activities by senior entrepreneurs in deprived communities are limited to personal commitments to members of the community. In some cases, their ventures may benefit the community by coincidence rather than choice, if the venture aligns with community values or services. The key factors hindering seniors' enterprising in deprived areas are of a personal nature, stemming principally from their own profession and flawed decision-making. The pursuit of entrepreneurial ambition in the chosen professional field is understandable as after many years spent in a particular profession or occupation senior entrepreneurs may feel uniquely qualified in a particular trade, which also may lead to a desire to be their own boss. Furthermore, they may think of themselves as sufficiently experienced to run a business without any formal training or relevant expertise. Altogether it suggests that senior entrepreneurs may feel embedded in a community, deprived or not. The task then is to realign their entrepreneurial orientation with the needs of the community.

LEARNING POINTS

- Training for professionals approaching their retirement age might significantly broaden their perspective on the range of activities available for them during retirement. Training how to launch and run a business would allow to link seniors' professional expertise with creative thinking about how to make use of the wealth of their knowledge for the benefit of the community, while emphasising contribution to the local welfare.
- Engaging seniors in community activism might serve as a stepping stone for nurturing their entrepreneurial skills. As many seniors are not looking to maximise financial gains, but rather to increase their satisfaction from life, launching a micro enterprise serving the needs of a deprived

community could be a logical next step for many, after donating their time for volunteer work in the local area.

- Many seniors would benefit from networking opportunities. These would allow them to learn about the needs of disadvantaged areas and populations, find out about how their contribution might address these needs and get acquainted with best practice, community activists and peers, leading to ideation regarding their future enterprise. Establishing a venture in a deprived area might face low or no competition, but advice and support from peers would allow to overcome the fear of unknown and bypass the society's (often) embedded perception of an entrepreneur as a younger person.

REFERENCES

Ainsworth, S. and Hardy, C. 2013. The enterprising self: an unsuitable job for an older worker, *Organization*, 15(3), 389–405.

Baucus, D.A. and Human, S.E. 1994. Second-career entrepreneurs: a multiple case study analysis of entrepreneurial processes and antecedent variables, *Entrepreneurship: Theory and Practice*, 19(2), 41–71.

Botham, R. and Graves, A. 2009. *The Grey Economy: How Third Age Entrepreneurs Are Contributing to Growth*, London, National Endowment for Science, Technology and the Arts (NESTA).

Crawford, A. and Naar, J. 2015. A profile of American bed and breakfast entrepreneurs: bridging the gap to retirement, *Journal of Human Resources in Hospitality & Tourism*, 15(1), 103–117.

Figueiredo, E. and Paiva, T. 2019. Senior entrepreneurship and qualified senior unemployment: the case of the Portuguese Northern region, *Journal of Small Business and Enterprise Development*, 26(3), 342–362.

Franck, A.K. 2010. I am too old! Who is going to give me a job? Women hawkers in Teluk Bahang, Penang, Malaysia, *Journal of Workplace Rights*, 15(1), 111–132.

Gray, H. 2007. Creating older entrepreneurs: a development dilemma, *Development and Learning in Organizations*, 21(1), 12–14.

Iparraguirre, J.L. 2018. *Economics and Ageing. Volume I: Theory*, Cham, Palgrave Macmillan.

Jurinski, J.J., Down, J. and Kolay, M. 2016. Helping older, encore entrepreneurs anticipate financial risks, *Journal of Financial Service Professionals*, 71(1), 81–90.

Kautonen, T. 2012. Do age-related social expectations influence entrepreneurial activity at older ages? *The International Journal of Entrepreneurship and Innovation*, 3(3), 179–187.

Kautonen, T., Down, S. and South, L. 2008. Enterprise support for older entrepreneurs: the case of PRIME in the UK, *International Journal of Entrepreneurial Behavior & Research*, 14(2), 85–101.

Kautonen, T., Hatak, I., Kibler, E. and Wainwright, T. 2015. Emergence of entrepreneurial behaviour: the role of age-based self-image, *Journal of Economic Psychology*, 50, 41–51.

Kenny, B. and Rossiter, I. 2018. Transitioning from unemployment to self-employment for over 50s, *International Journal of Entrepreneurial Behavior & Research*, 24(1), 234–255.

Kibler, E., Wainwright, T., Kautonen, T. and Blackburn, R. 2015. Can social exclusion against "older entrepreneurs" be managed? *Journal of Small Business Management*, 53(S1), 193–208.

Lévesque, M. and Minniti, M. 2006. The effect of aging on entrepreneurial behaviour, *Journal of Business Venturing*, 21(2), 177–194.

Lewis, K. and Walker, E. 2013. Third age self-employment: a business assistance perspective, *Journal of Small Business and Enterprise Development*, 20(2), 399–419.

Lin, S. and Wang, S. 2019. How does the age of serial entrepreneurs influence their re-venture speed after a business failure? *Small Business Economics*, 52(3), 651–666.

Martin, W.F. and Welsch, H. 2019. Wasted talent: battling exclusionary forces among senior entrepreneurs, *The International Journal of Entrepreneurship and Innovation*, 20(2), 130–143.

Nilsson, K. 2016. Conceptualisation of ageing in relation to factors of importance for extending working life – a review, *Scandinavian Journal of Public Health*, 44(5), 490–505.

OECD 2015. *Policy Brief on Expanding Networks for Inclusive Entrepreneurship*, Luxembourg, Publications Office of the European Union.

Perenyi, A., Zolin, R. and Maritz, A. 2018. The perceptions of Australian senior entrepreneurs on the drivers of their entrepreneurial activity, *International Journal of Entrepreneurial Behavior & Research*, 24(1), 81–103.

Ratten, V. 2019. Older entrepreneurship: a literature review and research agenda, *Journal of Enterprising*

Communities: People and Places in the Global Economy, 13(1/2), 178–195.

Sahut, J., Gharbi, S. and Mili, M. 2015. Identifying factors key to encouraging entrepreneurial intentions among seniors, *Canadian Journal of Administrative Sciences*, 32(4), 252–264.

Schøtt, T., Rogoff, E., Herrington, M. and Kew, P. 2017. *GEM Special Report on Senior Entrepreneurship 2017*, London, Global Entrepreneurship Research Association.

Singh, R. 2009. The aging population and mature entrepreneurs: market trends and implications for entrepreneurship, *New England Journal of Entrepreneurship*, 12(1), 45–53.

Skirbekk, V. 2008. Productivity potential during the life cycle: the changing importance of age-specific abilities, *Population and Development Review*, 34, 191–207.

Stirzaker, R.J. and Galloway, L. 2017. Ageing and redundancy and the silver lining of entrepreneurship, *The International Journal of Entrepreneurship and Innovation*, 18(2), 105–114.

Stirzaker, R. and Sitko, R. 2019. The older entrepreneurial self: intersecting identities of older women entrepreneurs, *International Journal of Entrepreneurial Behaviour & Research*, 25(8), 1748–1765. doi: 10.1108/ijebr-12-2017-0497

Stypińska, J. 2018. The enterprising self: a panacea for all or new fictitious social role for older adults? The analysis of European polices for senior entrepreneurship, *Journal of Population Ageing*, 11(1), 43–65.

Stypińska, J., Franke, A. and Myrczik, J. 2019. Senior entrepreneurship: the unrevealed driver for social innovation, *Frontiers in Sociology*, 4, 1–16. doi: 10.3389/fsoc.2019.00030

Tasner, P. 2017. *How I became an entrepreneur at 66* [Video file]. Available at: https://www.ted.com/talks/paul_tasner_how_i_became_an_entrepreneur_at_66

Verheul, I. and Van Mil, L. 2011. What determines the growth ambition of Dutch early-stage entrepreneurs? *International Journal of Entrepreneurial Venturing*, 3(2), 183–207.

Watkins-Mathys, L. 2012. Age and grey entrepreneurship. In *Lessons on Profiting from Diversity*, Ed. G. Moss, pp. 94–113, London, Palgrave Macmillan.

Weber, P. and Schaper, M. 2004. Understanding the grey entrepreneur, *Journal of Enterprising Culture*, 12(2), 147–164.

5

FOSTERING ENTREPRENEURSHIP IN COSMOPOLITAN CITIES*

INTRODUCTION

Political, economic, business and social processes in nations worldwide are influenced both by globalisation processes and growing cosmopolitanism. While globalisation should be viewed as more than simply an ability to engage in transactions across national borders (Spring, 2008), it is a process that has at least two dimensions: (a) external influences and (b) internal responses (Douglass, 2005). In processes, standardisation (i.e. standardised deployment of readily available solutions in politics, economics, commerce, banking, education, social structures and cultural approaches) prevails over nation-specific, contextually driven and culturally driven choices (Enders, 2004). In globalisation, worldwide trends dominate over locally rooted processes.

---

* The significant part of this chapter has been previously published as: Mouraviev and Kakabadse (2016).

In contrast to globalisation, cosmopolitanism allows individual values and individualised solutions, while actors including citizens, businesses, interest groups, governments and NGOs have a general agreement regarding diversity as a norm (Woodward et al., 2008). Paying respect to the differences and being fully aware of interdependence allows actors to create governance of diversity (Appiah, 2006). Globalisation and cosmopolitanism each have their own drivers and underlying dynamics. While globalisation is often driven by external impulses complemented by domestic policies, this chapter intends to contribute to a deeper conceptualisation of cosmopolitanism by analysing cities that have formed, or are forming, an environment that matches the cosmopolitanism' principal feature, i.e. governance of diversity for the common good. The chapter highlights the social norms and social forms that are critical for cosmopolitan cities and that cities create and benefit from.

Around the world, the cities and regions have shown significant variation in advancing entrepreneurship, promoting growth and ensuring economic, social and environmental sustainability. While city governments are keen, typically, on attracting investment, enhancing private enterprise and fostering economic growth, their success rates are different: some exhibit sustainable growth over lengthy periods, while the vulnerability of others shows their dependency on macroeconomic trends and changes in these trends. Cities with a largely cosmopolitan environment, such as Auckland, Berlin, Dubai, Edinburgh, Hong Kong, London, New York, Shanghai or Singapore, are successfully developing and attracting entrepreneurs from all over the world, even during the economic downturn (Sennett, 2002; Smith, 2007; Brooks, 2013; www.city-data.com). Naturally, these cities may also experience a level of economic decline during recession; however, their resilience to downward trends in their nation's economy is remarkably strong, and their ability to sustain entrepreneurship and growth remains high. This raises a host of questions regarding these cities' commonalities, and the reasons for their success. Are these cities cosmopolitan? What are the essential features of their environment that make it cosmopolitan? Furthermore, are there links between a cosmopolitan environment and effective urban development?

Why is this topic necessary for this book? What are the connections between cosmopolitanism, cosmopolitan cities and deprived communities? It seems that cosmopolitan cities, such as Auckland, London, New York and Shanghai, are prosperous and demonstrate resilience and growth. While it is true that these cities are more prosperous than many other, each of them has pockets of poverty and certain areas that have poorer neighbourhoods and concentration of disadvantaged people, such as unemployed, low-skilled and/or newly arrived immigrants looking for a job. These problematic areas present an ongoing challenge to urban governments as financially supporting disadvantaged groups could be costly for the cities' budget. In contrast, many cosmopolitan cities, much like other cities, would prefer a more sustainable way of poverty alleviation, that is, by enabling entrepreneurship in their deprived communities and offering opportunities to disadvantaged populations. The difference between cosmopolitan and other cities is that in a global city, entrepreneurship is typically a key driver of economic growth. Therefore, extending enterprise culture to deprived communities is natural and easier in a cosmopolitan environment.

The extant literature is silent regarding the relationship between cosmopolitanism, entrepreneurship, urban environment and sustainable development. While the body of knowledge about cosmopolitanism is growing, scholars attempt to conceptualise cosmopolitanism from certain angles including the sociological perspective, cultural adaptation or via studies of entrepreneurs who take advantage of networking opportunities that cosmopolitan environments offer (for example, see Jack et al., 2004; De Clercq and Voronov, 2009; Kendall et al.,2009; Delanty, 2012). However, the literature would benefit from comprehensive studies that provide a detailed account of the cosmopolitan environment's features and how they evolve, explain whether or not this environment fosters entrepreneurship and, ultimately, how it contributes to resilience of cosmopolitan urban areas. While cosmopolitanism may be observed in various environments, its most salient manifestations can be noted in large urban areas that demonstrate flourishing entrepreneurship, a large number of international firms, a high percentage of foreign-born resident population and foreign nationals who do business. Therefore, the gap that this chapter aims to address, at least in part, refers to the explanation of what constitutes a cosmopolitan city, how entrepreneurs perceive its traits and themselves in a cosmopolitan environment and, specifically, how entrepreneurs perceive and collaborate with the power holders. As city's development heavily depends upon entrepreneurship, this chapter's significance is justified by noting the existence of a direct link between sustainable urban growth and the cosmopolitan environment that feeds entrepreneurship.

This chapter argues that the unique character of certain urban areas makes them attractive to entrepreneurs from different nations, regardless of macroeconomic fluctuations in the business cycle. Furthermore, the distinct cosmopolitan environment of these urban areas ensures economic growth, via entrepreneurship, even in times of recession. Hence, an understanding of the interplay between cosmopolitanism and entrepreneurship is critical in identifying how cities can ensure sustainable development. Additionally, the factors that facilitate cosmopolitanism merit exploration. As each city has its own contextual environment, this suggests that cosmopolitanism is, inevitably, locally grounded, although one can hardly dispute its international orientation. While the urban context that contributes to cosmopolitanism deserves investigation from a variety of perspectives, for this chapter the authors have chosen the power perspective and, more specifically, the three-dimensional view of power (Lukes, 2005).

This chapter aims to conceptualise enablers of cosmopolitanism from the *third-level power perspective*, drawing on Lukes' theory of power (Lukes, 2005). Additionally, the chapter investigates the relationship between entrepreneurs' cosmopolitan dispositions and *habitus*, i.e. a pattern of an individual's demeanour, as conceptualised by Bourdieu (1977, 1990). The chapter makes use of Bourdieu's framework (*habitus*) by extending it to the urban cosmopolitan environment and linking habitus to the three-dimensional theory of power.

The chapter begins by highlighting the meaning of cosmopolitanism, cosmopolitan disposition and habitus. It then develops a theoretical model that enables an understanding of how power and the powerful shape cosmopolitanism and, ultimately, urban development via entrepreneurship. The chapter outlines the principal elements of a cosmopolitan disposition and the critical factors in influencing the powerful. The conclusion draws insights into how cosmopolitanism may become a more effective tool for entrepreneurship and urban development.

COSMOPOLITANISM AS AN IDENTITY, IDENTITY TRANSFORMATION AND VALUE

In conceptualising cosmopolitanism, we draw on Douzinas' (2007) view that cosmopolitanism forms an identity that is signified by an individual's departure from the fixed spatio-temporal dimension to the bigger world and that 'cosmopolitanism is about sameness, difference and values themselves' (Douzinas, 2007, p. 175). For example, cosmopolitan entrepreneurs exhibit similar behaviours, attitudes and a high degree of adaptability as they easily move from one location to another and take advantage of a favourable environment for doing business. They are naturally different from each other from the perspective of their educational and cultural background and how they do business, although it is likely that their perceptions of risk, opportunities and appropriate management practices are similar, as they show transnational, rather than domestic, orientation and learn from each other (Drori et al., 2009; Honig et al., 2010). As for values, cosmopolitanism forms a set of attitudes, behaviours and practices, among which society's openness to entrepreneurship is critical (Kendall et al., 2009). Other significant cosmopolitanism features are attitudes to, and appreciation of, human rights, social diversity, global environmental protection, consumption and aesthetics (Woodward et al., 2008). Furthermore, cosmopolitan values include social inclusion and tolerance (Jack et al., 2004; Honig et al., 2010).

While cosmopolitanism is, in Socrates' words, an identity of a 'citizen of the world' (Kakabadse and Kakabadse, 2012), it also implies identity transformation. Cosmopolitanism may involve the active construction of social forms that benefit cosmopolitan individuals. An example of these social forms is a power structure, such as a municipal agency charged with responsibility for urban development and attracting private investment. The agency's performance is likely to be assessed by the level of investment it brings to the city and how many companies are formed during a year. Therefore, in order to be successful, it has to provide benefits to entrepreneurs and create an environment that is attractive to not only businesses from its home country, but also to entrepreneurs from any other nation (Anderson et al., 2010; Honig et al., 2010; Igarashi and Saito, 2014). The construction of social forms that reinforce and enhance openness, behaviours (e.g. swift decision-making), attitudes (e.g. accepting diversity as a norm) and practices (e.g. CSR actions) may be viewed as the process of value creation, in which institutional structures evolve and strengthen a cosmopolitan disposition and cosmopolitan values (Woodward and Skrbiš, 2012). Hence, in a certain context, in which cosmopolitanism is a value, social structures become cosmopolitan (Beck, 2006) and work towards identity transformation. This furthers the urban area's cosmopolitan orientation, the core of which is transformation of identities, both human and organisational, in the direction of greater openness and an ever-increasing appreciation of cosmopolitan attitudes, behaviours and values.

Cosmopolitanism also implies *disposition* and *habitus*. The cosmopolitan disposition may be viewed as a habitual inclination or tendency to do things in a certain way, or to exhibit a certain pattern of behaviour that is aligned with openness and other cosmopolitan values. The cosmopolitan disposition is part of habitus, which is defined as the interplay of dispositions and structures over time (Bourdieu, 1984). Aristotle's concept of habitus, re-worked by Aquinas and revived by a sociologist (Mauss) and philosopher (Merleau-Ponty), has subsequently been advanced and used by sociologist and anthropologist Bourdieu as an analytical tool for understanding the cognitive components of action (Lizardo, 2004). Aristotle's notion of habitus is conceptualised as *hexis* (the Latin translation of a Greek word), which refers to the state of possessing (or 'having', Latin *habere*) an acquired, trained disposition to engage in certain modes of activity when encountering particular situations (Lizardo, 2004).

Habitus refers to how 'society becomes deposited in persons in the form of lasting dispositions, or trained capacities and structured propensities to think, feel and act in determinant ways, which then guide them' (Wacquant, 2005, p. 316). Bourdieu (1984) argues that habitus is created unconsciously over a lengthy period of time, 'without any deliberate pursuit of coherence... without any conscious concentration' (Bourdieu, 1984, p. 170). Bourdieu's habitus is the product of adaptation to a variety of conditions in the environment. Habitus implies that a person re-creates the very same conditions under which the set of skills and dispositions that are constitutive of it can be most profitably put to use. Conversely, habitus predisposes a person to avoid those environments and situations for which he is not well equipped. This is echoed by Brubaker (1993) who also notes a lack of deliberate actions in the formation of habitus by suggesting, 'habitus governs practice in a subconscious, unreflective manner' (Brubaker, 1993, p. 225). Nonetheless, Bourdieu (1984), Brubaker (1993) and Wacquant (2005) acknowledge that social structures play a certain role in shaping dispositions, and that habitus can change over time. Linking habitus to the three-dimensional theory of power (as discussed in the next section), we argue that social structures, such as entrepreneurial and power elites, are likely to play a growing role in the formation of cosmopolitan habitus, and conscious actions may significantly shape, strengthen or weaken the cosmopolitan environment in urban areas. The influence of social structures on cosmopolitan habitus depends on whether cosmopolitanism is embedded in society (or, more precisely, in a certain urban area) as its value and, if so, how deeply it is shared by the community.

THEORETICAL MODEL

This chapter makes use of Lukes' (1974, 2005) three-dimensional theory of power and connects it with the concepts of disposition and habitus in the cosmopolitan environment. Power refers to 'agents' abilities to bring about significant effects, specifically by furthering their own interests and/or affecting the interests of others, whether positively or negatively' (Lukes, 2005, pp. 64–65). One of the critical issues that Lukes (2005) investigates is how the powerful secure the willing compliance of those they dominate. The note about *willing* compliance is directly linked to the cosmopolitan environment and cosmopolitan mindset, as both cannot evolve without the voluntary engagement of entrepreneurs who are willing to do business internationally and are comfortable with moving around the world in order to take advantage of newly opened business opportunities.

The three-dimensional theory of power forms the conceptual foundation for this chapter. It draws specifically on the third dimension of power and applies power elite's preference-shaping capacity to the urban environment that demonstrates cosmopolitan features. Nourished by power holders, the cosmopolitan environment becomes an attractive and fruitful field for entrepreneurs who both benefit from this environment and contribute to furthering it. Entrepreneurs' disposition and habitus materialise in the cosmopolitan environment and become part of it, while the power holders use disposition in order to enhance habitus and transform entrepreneurs' acquiescence into willing compliance with the preferences established by the elite. Fig. 5.1 shows the key concepts that this chapter employs.

In the conceptualisation of power, its understanding as a capacity is of particular value for this chapter. This is because the capacity to produce a desired effect, adjust self-interests and influence the interests of others constitute the core of

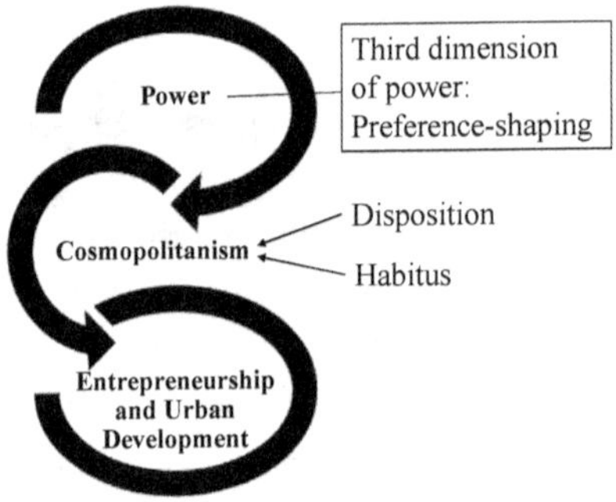

Source: Compiled by the authors.

Fig. 5.1. Key Concepts.

the three-dimensional view of power in which the third dimension – power as preference-shaping – appears critical for the formation of cosmopolitan habitus. The one-dimensional perspective suggests that power is *intentional and active* (i.e. hard and explicit power, coercive and observable), while the two-dimensional view acknowledges that power may also be seen as 'soft' as it is used for *agenda-setting* (i.e. power appears less visible, such as the power to influence) (Lukes, 2005). The three-dimensional view incorporates into the power relations the *preference-shaping* capacity of power (i.e. power is invisible and shapes preferences via values, norms and ideologies) (Lukes, 2005). One of the merits of the three-dimensional view is in its departure from the behavioural (i.e. individualistic) focus of power. Instead, this view incorporates social structures and institutional practices into power relations, as it focuses on issues and potential issues, observable and latent conflicts, and subjective and real interests (Lukes, 2005). While the three-dimensional view of power implies recognition that multiple, often competing, interests exist, it also implies that power holders must consider the interests of the dominated, and must deal with the dominated, in order to address their interests and/or to further own interests.

The three-dimensional theory of power facilitates the capture of the important details of the dominant–dominated relationship. Lukes (2005) calls it the 'supreme' exercise of power when the powerful secure the compliance of the dominated by influencing, shaping and determining their wants and thoughts. While controlling thoughts and desires may take a certain form of coercion, the easier and more effective power relations may stem from the *willing* compliance of the dominated. Normally, the latter, being subjected to dominance, would not have a choice but to acquiesce in their domination. This type of compliance does not involve the willingness of the dominated, and the implication for societal development is that, inevitably, the dominated adopt a passive role as they become disengaged from the objectives set by the power holders.

While Foucault (1980) rejects the notion that a central ordered and rational agency exists and regulates power, he also views powerlessness as a natural element structured into human existence. Foucault (1980, 1982) also asserts that there are no chances of bringing about social change through local efforts, and therefore acquiescence becomes an intrinsic feature of power relations. In contrast to this, Lukes (2005) argues that central authority does exist and the power holders can act rationally to adjust power relations with the powerless. The latter also, in Lukes' (2005) view, can act rationally and purposefully, and can engage in the promotion of certain preferences that suit them.

PREFERENCE-SHAPING TO PROMOTE ENTREPRENEURSHIP

In order to create a different type of compliance, the powerful may use their preference-shaping capacity to promote certain values and embed these values within social structures and institutional practices (Skrbiš and Woodward, 2013). The status of these values, as determined and reinforced by the powerful, is important because it shows to the dominated the value system of power holders, and where a certain value is positioned within the system. As the dominated may take on the values that justify their domination, they may actively promote these values by deliberate actions that further the values, institutionalise them and embed them in everyday life. This type of compliance presents a different kind of power relations that show a departure from mere acquiescence of the dominated. Instead, the dominated become actively engaged in enhancing, institutionalising and internalising the societal values shared by both the powerful and the powerless.

It is worth noting that, in terms of exercising power, the interests of the powerful should be viewed as dynamic and evolving. As they are subject to change, there is no canonical set of interests (Lukes, 2005) that would form a permanent stance of the powerful regarding their own desires and values and what values they want the dominated to appreciate and act upon. Neither is there a given set of tools that might be used to ensure continuous compliance of the dominated with the rules, values, standards and structures set by the powerful. While the interests of the latter evolve, they can be influenced, which demonstrates that power is value dependent. The application of the three-dimensional power theory to cosmopolitanism, therefore, shows that, if cosmopolitanism is valued by society or the community of a certain urban area, power can promote cosmopolitanism. This implies that cosmopolitan entrepreneurs (i.e. the dominated) may not only acquiesce in their domination, but also explicitly benefit from the comfortable urban environment that is favourable for doing business.

The evolving set of interests can be illustrated by Dubai's experience. For a number of years during the 1980s and

1990s, Dubai has been successfully developing its financial structure and institutions by inviting both domestic and foreign firms to set up their operations, and by expanding lending and all types of other financial operations. As a result, Dubai has transformed itself into the regional financial centre for both the Persian Gulf nations and for the benefit of local companies that engaged, among many projects, in massive residential and commercial construction in Dubai via the use of affordable financing. This created a win-win situation for Dubai's residents, who are 97% foreign-born and who are actively engaged in entrepreneurship (Brook, 2013). Multiple benefits for the cosmopolitan city included massive job creation in the financial sector, construction and related industries, which attracted a workforce from all over the world including hired staff and entrepreneurs; plentiful opportunities for investment in developers' business; and sustained economic growth over 20 years. The development of Dubai's financial services and construction has been further expanded by an additional act of critical importance – land reform. Since 2002, foreigners have been allowed to own real estate in Dubai, reform that Dubai has accomplished first among the Gulf nations (Brook, 2013). This radical change created a real estate market in Dubai, which was earlier non-existent as most of land was owned by sheikhs and all others were renters. Owing to the 2002 land reform, anyone can buy a property in Dubai; this has created a real estate boom and boosted inflow of entrepreneurs and investors in the country, while making Dubai more cosmopolitan. There is no doubt that the government's action plan evolved over time and this has resulted in considerable achievements in the form of a constant influx of entrepreneurs from many nations, and their growing contribution to Dubai's diversity and economic durability.

INTEGRATING COSMOPOLITANISM AND ENTREPRENEURSHIP INTO COMMUNITY VALUES

The deliberate actions of the powerful, intended to create an open entrepreneurial environment and supportive structures (e.g. effective regulatory agencies, streamlined licencing procedures and liberal and transparent tax regimes), form a platform for the willing compliance of the dominated. As such, they are likely to increase entrepreneurs' *voluntary* engagement with the cosmopolitan environment as the latter brings benefits to their business (Li, 2007; Thornton and Comberti, 2013). To summarise, being sponsored and formed by the powerful, and aligned with the interests of the dominated, an enhanced cosmopolitan disposition embeds itself in cosmopolitan habitus. This ultimately benefits the power holders via urban economic growth, and entrepreneurs by ensuring profits and sustainability to their business ventures (Dodd et al., 2014).

However, while initially the dominant-dominated relationship may be driven principally by the powerful, it may also be driven by the dominated. Keeping in mind that a distinct feature of cosmopolitan entrepreneurs is active opportunity identification on an international scale, their social and political activism (i.e. vigorous efforts to bring about change) becomes a strong force in influencing power holders. Complemented by their wealth and ability to mobilise human and financial resources worldwide, cosmopolitan entrepreneurs may challenge how the dominant political elite uses the third dimension of power, i.e. how parameters of debate and thinking are defined. While a group of entrepreneurs – the most successful, influential and networked – forms the cosmopolitan elite, the latter by itself, much like the powerful, can employ the third dimension of power, i.e. can actively engage in preference-shaping.

Cosmopolitan elite members, as well as all other cosmopolitan entrepreneurs, will be able and willing to shape interests, promote wants and practice their cosmopolitan disposition on their own accord, without the exercise of explicit power by the political elite (the first dimension of power) and/or a pre-determined agenda set by the powerful (the second dimension of power). Due to their own interest in enhancing an open environment and forming the most favourable regime for doing business, cosmopolitans may further this environment autonomously, without direct orders from the top (i.e. without the employment of the third dimension of power). However, they will be significantly more effective if the powerful can deliberately integrate cosmopolitanism into societal or community values as this would facilitate entrepreneurs' autonomous acts in the face of incentives set up by others. In the best-case scenario, the coordinated actions of the political elite and the cosmopolitan entrepreneurial elite might lead to the establishment of regional and global systems of governance (Held, 2003). The idea of emerging cosmopolitan-driven regional (and international) governance mechanisms is echoed by the notion that cosmopolitanism and, more specifically, cosmopolitan entrepreneurs should be viewed as an evolving institutional structure (Douzinas, 2007). This structure has a significant capacity to influence political elite and power holders and engage in preference-shaping in order to promote a cosmopolitan mindset. This is how – through shaping and furthering values and their subsequent institutionalisation – the capacity of the powerless merges with that of the powerful. Not only do the power holders exert their influence, but also they are influenced by the dominated via the same kind of social processes that are embedded in the third dimension of power.

The three-dimensional power framework is useful as it demonstrates that a paradigm shift is required for the effective development of cosmopolitan areas. Instead of (or in addition to) exercising dominance, explicit power and agenda-setting, the powerful should promote values that will be shared by the dominated. Preference-shaping, rather than domination, will facilitate the transition of the powerless from acquiescence to active engagement with the very values that the powerful prefer (Lukes, 2005; Sova et al., 2015). This forms a cycle of influence where the dominated, through the entrepreneurial elite, become able to exert influence on power holders and further enhance the latter's preference-shaping capacity and practice for the benefit of the dominated, the powerful and the community at large (Li, 2007; Sova et al., 2015). Hence, repeat cycles of influence are required in order to ensure the successful advancement of shared values that make cosmopolitan cities' environments most favourable for doing business.

Fig. 5.2 demonstrates how this chapter's model evolved as compared to the initial concept reflected in Fig. 5.1. While Fig. 5.1 calls attention to the third dimension of power as the theoretical lens for this chapter, Fig. 5.2 emphasises what power's preference-shaping capacity can accomplish – it

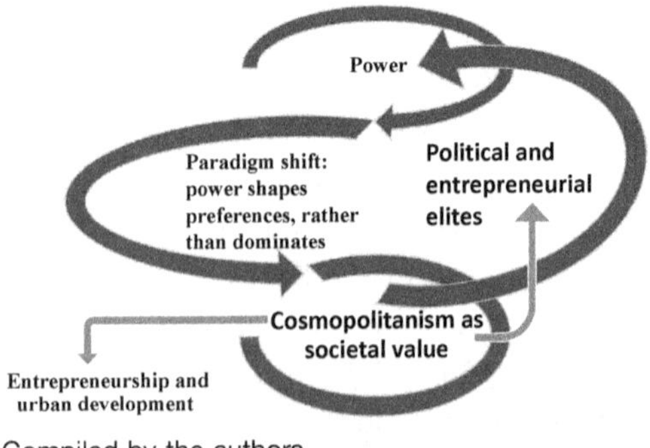

Source: Compiled by the authors.

Fig. 5.2. How Power Promotes Cosmopolitanism.

ensures a paradigm shift from one preference to another (or to an enhanced version of the original preference). By adjusting and furthering a community's preferences, which also cater, fully or in part, to the wants and needs of the powerless, the power elite departs from mere domination. Fig. 5.1 shows that cosmopolitanism is the foundation of the power elite's purposeful actions. Fig. 5.2 captures an enhanced conceptualisation of cosmopolitanism as a category that brings mutual benefits – to entrepreneurs, residents, community and society at large in the form of business opportunities, durable growth and stability. Therefore, Fig. 5.2 pictures cosmopolitanism in terms of societal value, rather than a mere description of the urban environment. Fig. 5.2 also demonstrates that cosmopolitanism as a shared societal value requires nurturing and enhancement both by power holders and the entrepreneurial elite, which assures that interests of both will be served, and this will lead to the subsequent cycles of adjustment. To reiterate, the cycle of adjustment includes the capture of:

- Cosmopolitanism-generated influences on power holders and business people;
- Incorporation of these influences in power structures and processes;
- Further institutionalisation in the business environment and entrepreneurial attitudes and practices; and
- Reflection of newly adopted shared values in an evolved and updated understanding of cosmopolitanism by the vast majority of a certain urban community.

Fig. 5.2 displays the theoretical conceptual model that this chapter has developed.

COSMOPOLITAN DISPOSITION, NETWORKS AND INFLUENCING THE POWERFUL

While earlier the chapter conceptualised cosmopolitanism as identity and identity transformation, this suggests that the cosmopolitan disposition evolves and can be viewed as a never-ending process (De Clercq and Voronov, 2009; Skrbiš and Woodward, 2013). This raises a question regarding the key elements of the cosmopolitan disposition and the elements of a cosmopolitan disposition that are critical for influencing the powerful.

As this chapter views entrepreneurship in select urban areas through cosmopolitan habitus, this means that the entrepreneurs' milieu, i.e. the person's environment, determines the cosmopolitan disposition and the logic that motivates an individual to engage in creative business practice (Bourdieu, 1990; Woodward and Skrbiš, 2012). The entrepreneurs' milieu (environment) can be conceptualised as the logic of the field that determines the skills, traits and motivation that a cosmopolitan agent needs to have in order to be successful in the field (Delanty, 2006; Drori et al., 2009). However, the logic of the field should not be understood as a prerequisite for entering the field. An entrepreneur who lacks certain skills or traits still can benefit from the cosmopolitan milieu, and even contribute to its further strengthening, by adopting a cosmopolitan disposition and striving to practice it (Woodward et al., 2008; De Clercq and Voronov, 2009). As this chapter's theoretical model argues, a cosmopolitan disposition should not be treated as a given set of rules, norms and values. It can be influenced by the powerful and the values that power holders embed in their milieu and can also influence the power elites and their preference-shaping.

The cosmopolitan disposition includes core features, such as opportunity identification, and non-core, i.e. less critical features for the field's logic. An example of the latter is educational background (i.e. a specific academic degree) that does not play a critical role in the formation and adoption of a cosmopolitan mindset and in applying it to entrepreneurial practice. Table 5.1 highlights core characteristics of the cosmopolitan disposition and how they relate to the logic of the field (i.e. the entrepreneurial environment).

Table 5.1 shows the linkages between an entrepreneur and the urban environment across four dimensions: personal

Table 5.1. Entrepreneurs' Cosmopolitan Disposition: Core Features.

	Entrepreneurs' Cosmopolitan Disposition	The City's Milieu: Logic of the Field
Individual traits (agent's behavioural pattern)	High degree of motivation, self-reliance and adaptability	Integrity and trust (trustworthy business relations)
Structure	Active engagement in opportunity identification	Networks (professional, business, social and political)
Engagement with milieu	Orientation on multi-layered contribution to the urban environment	Respect for the city's social and cultural environment
Cultural identity	Focus on own identity – an individual as part of the world	Tolerance to cultural differences (i.e. co-existence)

Source: Compiled by the authors.

traits, structure, engagement with the environment and cultural identity. For example, the first dimension – individual traits that form an entrepreneur's behavioural pattern – emphasises a high degree of motivation and adaptability, which is typical for entrepreneurs. At the level of the city, these traits transform into trustworthy business relations, which is a feature of the cosmopolitan environment, and this is how entrepreneurs' individual traits are embedded in the urban cosmopolitan milieu. In other words, entrepreneurs' disposition that was noted in Fig. 5.1 links with the cosmopolitanism of the urban area (Fig. 5.2) and forms habitus as the product of adaptation to conditions in the environment, which is reflected in Table 5.1 as the city's milieu. An additional example can be drawn from the second dimension, which captures links between an entrepreneur and milieu at the level of structures and institutions. As entrepreneurs are usually actively engaged in opportunity identification (cosmopolitan disposition in Fig. 5.1), in the urban cosmopolitan environment this transforms into extensive networking that creates shared value (see Fig. 5.2) and reveals business opportunities for the benefit of both entrepreneurs and a city (the urban milieu in Table 5.1). This is the case in many cities, including Dubai, New York and Shanghai.

As cosmopolitan habitus – the logic of the entrepreneurs' milieu – may have varying manifestations in different nations due to unique interplay of cultural traits, government regulations and business practices in a certain economic, social and spatial setting, the critical significance of the urban area's context for the formation of a cosmopolitan mindset must be emphasised. Still, it is likely that the core elements of disposition remain the same across cosmopolitan areas. As Table 5.1 shows, an entrepreneur's cosmopolitan mindset is closely aligned with the logic of the field (i.e. rules of the city's environment) along four dimensions, which demonstrates the high degree of integration. Hence, a cosmopolitan disposition strengthens entrepreneurial orientation, while the latter ensures a continuous inflow of newcomers to the field, who benefit from its cosmopolitan nature and also contribute to its advancement.

The cosmopolitan disposition's feature that ensures an entrepreneur's ability to influence the powerful is active engagement in opportunity identification. Often opportunities appear as a result of personal interaction with other businesses, government officials and customers. Table 5.1 shows that opportunity identification is linked to networks, a critical feature of the cosmopolitan city's milieu (Anderson et al., 2005, 2010). Being integrated with commercial, financial and political networks not only provides an entrepreneur with access to opportunities and resources, but also legitimises an entrepreneur in the cosmopolitan setting as an agent who receives influence from the powerful, and who is embedded in the cosmopolitan networks that are capable of exerting influence on power holders (Anderson et al., 2005, 2010; Jack et al., 2008; Igarashi and Saito, 2014).

This is supported by the notion that entrepreneurs need to concurrently 'fit in' the entrepreneurial process and 'stand out' (De Clercq and Voronov, 2009). Extending this notion, this chapter argues that the cosmopolitan environment requires that entrepreneurs legitimise themselves by conforming, in Bourdieu's terminology, to the logic of the field along two critical dimensions. One is engagement in networking; the other is the exercise of the cosmopolitan influence by active preference-shaping. Conforming to the two dimensions ensures that an entrepreneur concurrently 'fits in' and 'stands out'. Acceptance to the networks ensures entrepreneurs' conformity with existing practices and provides them with an opportunity and channels to exert influence on political and business elites. Hence, networks should be viewed as a critical part of milieu and the medium to influence that milieu.

The chapter has applied the three-dimensional view of power, with an emphasis on its preference-shaping dimension, to the cosmopolitan setting of select urban areas and highlighted how the cosmopolitan environment benefits both entrepreneurs and power holders. While the chapter sought to conceptualise the drivers of the development of cosmopolitan areas from the power perspective, revisiting the chapter's theoretical framework will now enable us to assess whether it was appropriate in serving the research aim. The chapter offers a theoretical model that develops Lukes' (2005) work and appears adequate and instrumental: it enriches the understanding of the power-cosmopolitanism-entrepreneurship link by emphasising the preference-shaping capacity of power, which leads to the embedment of cosmopolitanism in societal values. As a value shared by political and business elites, cosmopolitanism is appreciated and, importantly, actively promoted by entrepreneurs through their disposition and habitus, which ensures not only their willing compliance with power and the milieu, but also their enhancement of favourable business conditions. Entrepreneurs depart from mere acquiescence (to power and its explicit dominance) towards practising their cosmopolitan influence by active preference-shaping. Once cosmopolitanism is embedded in societal (or – more precisely – the urban area's) values, this creates multiple endless rounds of mutual influence (by power holders onto entrepreneurs via political and business elites, and by entrepreneurs onto power holders via the same channels), with mutual benefit. Therefore, mutually beneficial influence that transpires in continuous support of a cosmopolitan city's environment may be viewed as one of the factors that enhance cosmopolitan cities' resilience to changes in macroeconomic conditions. Hence, the theoretical perspective taken by the chapter appears appropriate and useful for confirming the existence of a link between the cosmopolitan environment and sustainable growth: cosmopolitanism feeds entrepreneurship and, through the latter, may significantly contribute to sustainable urban development including revitalising deprived areas.

CONCLUSION

Cosmopolitanism may be viewed as a value not only by entrepreneurs who look for business opportunities around the globe, but also by power holders. The latter may have a high and ever-increasing appreciation of cosmopolitanism for two reasons. First, to an urban area they would welcome entrepreneurs with a cosmopolitan mindset as they facilitate investment, create jobs and increase the region's output. Second, transnational entrepreneurs are those individuals who actively promote cosmopolitanism as a value and, in this capacity, they show not only acquiescence to power structures, but also a willing compliance with existing processes and the desire to improve these processes for their own and common good. This reason may have special significance for power holders as they can fully exercise their third dimension of power, i.e. preference-shaping, for the benefit of society or an area: if cosmopolitanism is valued, power and its holders can further promote cosmopolitanism.

Preference-shaping appears central to the identification of growth drivers in cosmopolitan areas as it manifests itself twice:

- Cosmopolitanism will be most effective when cosmopolitan belief structures are intentionally set by others, i.e. power holders, and

- As cosmopolitan entrepreneurs may gradually become part of the powerful elite, they can, therefore, increase their own influence on shaping preferences.

While not every entrepreneur can be considered to be in possession of a cosmopolitan mindset, the importance of networks should not be overlooked. Networks are critical for legitimising cosmopolitan entrepreneurs, as networks are part of milieu and the medium to influence that milieu (Anderson et al., 2005, 2010; Jack et al., 2008). The significance that is attached to networks is aligned with the concept of habitus: cosmopolitanism through international networks contributes towards creating a way of perceiving and acting in the world (i.e. a form of habitus), which facilitates transformation from local to expanded (worldwide) space (Tragardh, 2007).

The chapter's conclusion on the significance of preference-shaping in developing and institutionalising cosmopolitan environment has a broader implication of a practical nature for government economic policy. As preference-shaping is driven by government's long-term political and economic agendas, often economic growth and associated income distribution lie at the core of that government choice. Therefore, cosmopolitanism that leads to sustainable entrepreneurship and steady economic growth may be a preferred solution for urban and/or regional development and poverty alleviation, once the power holders demonstrate their political will to engage with cosmopolitanism as a value. Further, cosmopolitanism as a shared value might be used as a tool for political governance: as a common platform that unites power holders, business elites and an urban community at large, including disadvantaged populations in less prosperous areas, cosmopolitanism may ensure a fairer power balance in which voices of entrepreneurs, and the elites that represent them, may be heard and acted upon.

It is worth acknowledging the limitations of this chapter. One of them includes the lack of empirical studies to support the chapter's observations and conclusions, although a recent book on entrepreneurship in global cities (see Mouraviev and Kakabadse, 2020) should be noted as a contribution to the field. There is also insufficient research into both what constitutes a cosmopolitan city, and how the urban environment interacts with cosmopolitan entrepreneurs. Although cosmopolitan cities have been steadily growing and displaying economic and social durability over recent decades, the properties of co-evolution (entrepreneurs and the urban area) have yet to be studied, which might shed more light on cities' resilience and sustainability. Future research might investigate the interaction between cosmopolitanism and power elites in urban areas and test the conceptual conclusions of this chapter. Useful research themes might include the study of the links between the power elite and business elites, how they interact and the tools they use in order to exercise their preference-shaping capacity to promote entrepreneurship in urban areas including deprived communities.

LEARNING POINTS

- Certain urban areas draw distinct benefits from their cosmopolitan environment that fosters entrepreneurship and, ultimately, ensures sustainable economic growth. Although some neighbourhoods in these cities are affluent, other areas might be deprived, and the interplay between cosmopolitanism and entrepreneurship is critical for furthering overall economic development of the city.
- The urban area's cosmopolitan orientation implies transformation of identities, both human and organisational, in the

direction of greater openness and an ever-increasing appreciation of cosmopolitan attitudes, behaviours and values.

- Experience of global cities shows that cosmopolitanism will be most effective for furthering entrepreneurship when cosmopolitan belief structures are intentionally set by power holders. This presents a task for urban governing bodies – to promote openness, diversity as a norm and opportunity identification to make sure that aspiring entrepreneurs take advantage of these conditions by implementing their business projects, and, therefore, contributing to revitalisation of deprived communities via job creation and income generation.
- As a shared value, cosmopolitanism could be used for uniting power holders, business elites, social activists and an urban community at large, including disadvantaged populations in less prosperous areas, as cosmopolitan environment may ensure a fairer power balance in which voices of entrepreneurs, and the elites that represent them, may be heard and acted upon.

REFERENCES

Anderson, A.R., Drakopoulou Dodd, S. and Jack, S.L. 2005. The role of family members in entrepreneurial networks: beyond the boundaries of the family firm, *Family Business Review*, 2(18), 135–154.

Anderson, A.R., Drakopoulou Dodd, S. and Jack, S.L. 2010. Network practices and entrepreneurial growth, *Scandinavian Journal of Management*, 26(2), 121–133.

Appiah, K.H. 2006. *Cosmopolitanism: Ethics in a World of Strangers*, London, Penguin.

Beck, U. 2006. *Cosmopolitan Vision*, Cambridge, Polity Press.

Bourdieu, P. 1977. *Outline of a Theory of Practice*, Cambridge, Cambridge University Press.

Bourdieu, P. 1984. *Distinction: A Social Critique of the Judgement of Taste*, Cambridge, MA, Harvard University Press.

Bourdieu, P. 1990. *The Logic of Practice*, Stanford, CA, Stanford University Press.

Brook, D. 2013. How Dubai became Dubai, Next City. Available at: https://nextcity.org/daily/entry/how-dubai-became-dubai

Brubaker, R. 1993. Social theory as habitus. In *Bourdieu: Critical Perspectives*, Eds C. Calhoun, E. LiPuma and M. Postone, pp. 212–234, Chicago, IL, University of Chicago Press.

De Clercq, D. and Voronov, M. 2009. The role of cultural and symbolic capital in entrepreneurs' ability to meet expectations about conformity and innovation, *Journal of Small Business Management*, 47(3), 398–420.

Delanty, G. 2006. The cosmopolitan imagination: critical cosmopolitanism and social theory, *British Journal of Sociology*, 57(1), 25–47.

Delanty, G. Ed. 2012. *Handbook of Cosmopolitanism Studies*, pp. 127–137, London, Routledge.

Dodd, S., McDonald, S., McElwee, G. and Smith, R. 2014. A Bourdieuan analysis of qualitative authorship in entrepreneurship scholarship, *Journal of Small Business Management*, 52(4), 633–654.

Douglass, J. 2005. How all globalization is local: countervailing forces and their influence on higher education markets, *Higher Education Policy*, 18(4), 445–473.

Douzinas, C. 2007. *Human Rights and Empire: The Political Philosophy of Cosmopolitanism*, New York, NY, Routledge-Cavendish.

Drori, I., Honig, B. and Wright, M. 2009. Transnational entrepreneurship: an emergent field of study, *Entrepreneurship: Theory and Practice*, 33(5), 1001–1022.

Enders, J. 2004. Higher education, internationalization, and the nation-state: recent developments and challenges to governance theory, *Higher Education*, 47(3), 361–382.

Foucault, M. 1980. *Power/Knowledge: Selected Interviews and Other Writings, 1972–1977*, New York, NY, Pantheon Books.

Foucault, M. 1982. The subject and power, *Critical Inquiry*, 8(4), 777–795.

Held, D. 2003. Violence, law and justice in a global age. In *Debating Cosmopolitics*, Ed. D. Archibugi, London, Verso.

Honig, B., Drori, I. and Carmichael, B. Eds 2010. *Transnational and Immigrant Entrepreneurship in a Globalized World*, Toronto, ON, University of Toronto Press.

Igarashi, H. and Saito, H. 2014. Cosmopolitanism as cultural capital: exploring the intersection of globalization, education and stratification, *Cultural Sociology*, 8(3), 222–239.

Jack, S.L., Dodd, S.D. and Anderson, A.R. 2004. Social structures and entrepreneurial networks: the strength of strong ties, *The International Journal of Entrepreneurship and Innovation*, 5(2), 107–120.

Jack, S., Dodd, S.D. and Anderson, A.R. 2008. Change and the development of entrepreneurial networks over time: a processual perspective, *Entrepreneurship & Regional Development*, 20(2), 125–159.

Kakabadse, A. and Kakabadse, N. 2012. *Global Elites: The Opaque Nature of Transnational Policy Determination*, London, Palgrave Macmillan.

Kendall, G., Woodward, I. and Skrbiš, Z. 2009. *The Sociology of Cosmopolitanism*, London, Palgrave Macmillan.

Li, T.M. 2007. *The Will to Improve: Governmentality, Development, and the Practice of Politics*, Durham, NC, Duke University Press.

Lizardo, O. 2004. The cognitive origins of Bourdieu's habitus, *Journal for the Theory of Social Behaviour*, 34(4), 375–401.

Lukes, S. 1974. *Power: A Radical View*, Basingstoke, Macmillan.

Lukes, S. 2005. *Power: A Radical View*, 2nd ed., New York, NY, Palgrave Macmillan.

Mouraviev, N. and Kakabadse, N. 2016. Conceptualising cosmopolitanism and entrepreneurship through the lens of the three-dimensional theory of power. *Society and Business Review*, 11(3), 242–256.

Mouraviev, N. and Kakabadse, N. Eds 2020. *Entrepreneurship and Global Cities: Diversity, Opportunity and Cosmopolitanism*, New York, NY, Routledge.

Sennett, R. 2002. Cosmopolitanism and the social experience of cities. In *Conceiving Cosmopolitanism*, Eds S. Vertovec and R. Cohen, Oxford, Oxford University Press.

Skrbiš, Z. and Woodward, I. 2013. *Cosmopolitanism: Uses of the Idea*, London, SAGE Publications.

Smith, W. 2007. Cosmopolitan citizenship: virtue, irony and worldliness, *European Journal of Social Theory*, 10(1), 37–52.

Sova, C., Vervoort, J., Thornton, T., Helfgott, A., Matthews, D. and Chaudhury, A. 2015. Exploring farmer preference shaping in international agricultural climate change adaptation regimes, *Environmental Science & Policy*, 54, 463–474.

Spring, J. 2008. Research on globalization and education, *Review of Educational Research*, 78(2), 330–363.

Thornton, T. and Comberti, C. 2013. Synergies and trade-offs between adaptation, mitigation and development, *Climatic Change*, 140, 5–18. doi: 10.1007/s10584-013-0884-3

Tragardh, L. Ed. 2007. *State and Civil Society in Northern Europe: The Swedish Model Reconsidered*, Oxford, Berghanh Books.

Wacquant, L. 2005. Habitus. In *International Encyclopaedia of Economic Sociology*, Eds J. Becket and Z. Milan, London, Routledge.

Woodward, I., Skrbiš, Z. and Bean, C. 2008. Attitudes toward globalization and cosmopolitanism: cultural diversity, personal consumption and the national economy, *British Journal of Sociology*, 59(2), 207–226.

Woodward, I. and Skrbiš, Z. 2012. Performing cosmopolitanism. In *Handbook of Cosmopolitanism Studies*, Ed. G. Delanty, pp. 127–137, London, Routledge.

6

SOCIAL AND COMMUNITY-CENTRED ENTREPRENEURSHIP: DEVELOPING OPPORTUNITIES FOR DEPRIVED COMMUNITIES

INTRODUCTION

This chapter investigates approaches to revitalising deprived communities from a somewhat unusual perspective. This perspective is social entrepreneurship. As a field of research, social entrepreneurship has evolved relatively recently and is still in its infancy (Certo and Miller, 2008; Choi and Majumdar, 2014). In contrast to entrepreneurship that focuses on economic wealth, social entrepreneurship incorporates for-profit, nonprofit and hybrid forms of value creation to address social problems (Austin et al., 2006; Bacq and Janssen, 2011; Moss et al., 2011; Janssen et al., 2018). This chapter adopts an operational definition of social entrepreneurship as a process where a small or medium-sized business makes profit and uses part or all of it for social goals, such as supporting certain populations and/or local communities or meeting a specific social need (such as supporting displaced people or providing training). Another common type of social entrepreneurship is when a business hires staff from vulnerable and/or disadvantaged groups of society and/or people with disabilities and, therefore, likely gives up some labour productivity and profit. Although there might be other forms of social entrepreneurship, a critical criterion is that a company should be in business for profit (Lyon and Sepulveda, 2009).

Whilst this book emphasises the need to form and advance entrepreneurial culture, social entrepreneurship does not instantly appear as a tool that fits this purpose. One might think that entrepreneurship is more important than social entrepreneurship as the former creates jobs and generates income, which is the pathway for poverty reduction and prosperity. Naturally, entrepreneurship is a powerful tool for making communities prosperous; however, it typically develops well when an entrepreneurial ecosystem is already in place and it offers a set of favourable conditions, such as availability of low-cost financing options, supportive government structures and relatively high purchasing power of potential customers. However, if these conditions are missing, social entrepreneurship could play an important role by bringing to the fore the need and certain tools for community development.

The chapter discusses benefits that community-centred entrepreneurship could bring for the deprived areas making use of the results of the authors' study in Ukraine where a broad range of organisations engage in projects with social purpose. The study investigates aims, forms and models of existing socially focused entrepreneurial projects, interactions between enterprises and their communities, emphasising how economic activities of disadvantaged groups could be developed. Within this theme, the chapter identifies impact on advancing entrepreneurial culture that is the core framework for reinvigorating deprived communities.

The chapter begins by highlighting Ukraine's context in which poor economic conditions and ongoing military conflict play key roles. This is followed by the data collection details and who the participants of the study were. The chapter then proceeds by discussing the impact of socially focused entrepreneurship on community development. The conclusion compares different methods of enhancing entrepreneurial culture in deprived communities.

THE CONTEXT

Why was Ukraine chosen for this study? An ex-Soviet country, Ukraine has been transitioning to a market economy since it gained independence in 1991. The transition appeared lengthy and difficult, accompanied by the disruption of economic links, slow development of private enterprise and high unemployment. Independent Ukraine inherited from the Soviet Union a potent energy sector, a very good (although rapidly becoming outdated) infrastructure, a highly productive agriculture, as well as an educated workforce. However, the economy has been largely unstable and underperforming for almost 30 years. Ukraine's economy is represented mostly by heavy industry that is energy- and resource-intensive (Mouraviev and Koulouri, 2019). A large coal mining sector is inefficient and unprofitable, despite the economy being highly dependent on coal as an energy source. Ukraine is now the poorest country in Europe; incomes are low, and many people have been experiencing declining income in recent years, particularly since 2014. Data of the International Monetary Fund (IMF) show that Ukraine replaced Moldova as the poorest country in Europe: Ukraine's Gross Domestic Product (GDP) per capita in 2017 was as low as USD 2,655 vs USD 2,726 in Moldova

(International Monetary Fund, 2019). Ukraine's GDP per capita in 2018 is assessed at USD 2,963, 8% less than in Moldova.

Economic Conditions

The *Index of Economic Freedom*, compiled by the Heritage Foundation, Washington's think tank, shows that Ukraine's economic freedom score is 52.3, making its economy the 147th freest in the 2019 Index (The Heritage Foundation, 2019). The Heritage Foundation defines economic freedom as the fundamental right of every human to control his or her own labour and property. 'In an economically free society, individuals are free to work, produce, consume, and invest in any way they please. In economically free societies, governments allow labor, capital, and goods to move freely, and refrain from coercion or constraint of liberty beyond the extent necessary to protect and maintain liberty itself' (The Heritage Foundation, 2019). Although it is not widely accepted as a standard assessment of conditions supporting free enterprise, the Index nonetheless provides a useful description of the overall conditions in a country. The 2019 Index notes a small increase in the score for Ukraine owing to improvements in fiscal health, business freedom and property rights. However, the score also reflects decline in labour freedom and trade freedom. Ukraine is ranked the lowest among 44 countries in the Europe region, and its overall score is below the regional and world averages (The Heritage Foundation, 2019). To summarise, the Index is the reflection of Ukraine's very difficult, largely unfavourable conditions for developing entrepreneurship including its social dimension whilst the need for job creation and income generation to revitalise poor areas and support disadvantaged populations is fast growing.

Ongoing Military Conflict

The conflict with Russia, which began in 2014, has had a significant impact on the nation's economy and politics. The conflict resulted in the annexation of the Ukrainian Crimea (a peninsula in the Black Sea) by Russia. It also resulted in the loss of control over considerable parts of Donetsk and Luhansk *oblasts* (provinces), two territories, also known as Donbas, in the east of the country. In Donbas, where over 80% of Ukrainian coal mining takes place, in 2014 two regions – the Donetsk oblast and the Luhansk oblast– declared themselves independent nations (i.e. independent from Ukraine) and renamed themselves as Donetsk People's Republic (DPR) and Luhansk People's Republic (LPR). The two breakaway regions are populated mostly by ethnic Russians and are supported by Russia that renders all kinds of assistance including military, although neither Russia, nor Ukraine nor the international community have recognised the regions as independent nations. Since 2014, there is an ongoing military standoff on the border of these regions with the rest of Ukraine, in which shooting from both sides and other military operations take place almost on a daily basis. To date, the conflict has resulted in dozens of casualties on both sides, with a growing number of lost lives and casualties. Ukraine has significant military presence at the front line aiming to at least control the border and in the long run regain the breakaway territories. During the five-year duration of this military conflict (that many in Ukraine call a war) thousands of military personnel participated in combat operations and, upon completion of their service, were discharged.

Vulnerable Populations

The armed conflict with Russia continues to damage the Ukrainian society. As a result of the conflict, two disadvantaged groups have been formed and keep growing in size – displaced people and the veterans. There are more than two million internally displaced people who lost their homes and jobs in Donbas as they were effectively forced to move to other areas in Ukraine. Their demand for accommodation remains very high, whilst many of them are unemployed, which further aggravates their ability to purchase or rent housing. Scattered across Ukraine, internally displaced people form a very large group of disadvantaged individuals who require support. Without support, displaced people are likely to contribute to deprivation of communities as the livelihood of many has been damaged and in many cases they do not have any reliable means to take care of basic living expenses.

Another vulnerable group is the veterans. The armed conflict in the east of Ukraine has direct relevance to this chapter as it discusses entrepreneurship by veterans of this conflict and shows how veterans' business can support this vulnerable community and in essence forms the entrepreneurial ecosystem for them, whilst also demonstrates an example of social entrepreneurship. After completing military service, veterans who are typically young men in their 20s or early 30s return to civilian life and need to reintegrate. Finding an office job in a poorly performing economy with high unemployment is a challenging task and not a feasible option for most veterans, therefore many are looking for opportunities to start their own businesses. However, veterans can face considerable difficulties reintegrating into society as they are disturbed by their experience of violence, life-threatening situations, and moral and physical pressure. Even those who are interested in launching their own business struggle to connect with other people owing to the sharp difference in mindsets. The difficulties of reintegration often result in unemployment among veterans and affect their ability to become entrepreneurs. Veterans often engage with their own communities, in the form of local associations and the national network, mostly as a forum for socialisation. Consisting mainly of unemployed and self-isolated veterans, these local communities are characterised by poverty and deprivation, which create fertile grounds for the use of drugs and the growth of crime. Helping these communities to overcome deprivation is a challenging task, whilst developing entrepreneurship may be one of the powerful tools for improving veterans' livelihood.

In the conditions of a generally unbalanced and weak economy and distressed society (which is manifested by an ongoing armed conflict, high unemployment, growing poverty, no social care to support those in need, etc.), Ukraine is currently experiencing a genuine boom in social entrepreneurship where firms, mostly small, make profit and also pursue a social purpose. Although a detailed identification of the reasons that enable active social entrepreneurship in modern Ukraine is beyond this chapter's scope, noting that social entrepreneurship is a well-known concept and well-established practice in a nation torn by the military conflict is important in order to understand the study's context. As this chapter shows, social entrepreneurship could be instrumental in developing entrepreneurship.

Decentralisation

Another essential feature of Ukraine's context is the country's ongoing political and economic decentralisation. The programme of reforms has been approved by Ukraine's national parliament in 2014 and is being implemented. The reforms' core is creation of local communities (*hromada* in Ukrainian) and enabling them to better meet the needs of local residents. The ultimate purpose is to empower communities, foster economic development, create jobs and form better conditions for entrepreneurship at the local level. Although the ability of local authorities to create jobs is often limited, they may be more influential and successful in formation of entrepreneurial culture in the communities. This culture, complemented by support programmes and conditions favourable for business venture creation, should be viewed as a core element for developing entrepreneurship. Whilst in prosperous areas this culture's role is likely to be less important due to already established enterprises showing success, in deprived communities where jobs are scarce and the number of businesses is very small, nurturing entrepreneurial culture and providing support to emergent ventures become critical for economic development and poverty alleviation.

Why is decentralisation important for this chapter's theme? Since 2014, when implementation of decentralisation reforms began, many examples became available where local authorities initiated a range of programmes aimed at developing entrepreneurship. Working in concert with NGOs, volunteers and businesses, local authorities in the decentralisation context are considerably more interested in supporting all kinds of entrepreneurial projects as long as they create jobs, generate tax revenue and contribute to local area's development. In other words, decentralisation reform made local authorities responsible for advancing entrepreneurship in their areas and more responsive to business initiatives with social purpose. In part, this explains why Ukraine's social entrepreneurship is currently developing so fast.

THE STUDY

This study focused on investigation of impact that Ukraine's social entrepreneurship has on revitalisation of deprived communities. The analysis is based on 16 in-depth interviews with Ukraine's social activists, NGO leaders and participants, small business owners, social entrepreneurs and officials in the local authorities. Some study participants are university lecturers, and they are actively involved in projects with the social purpose, in addition to their university jobs. Most of the participants reside in Kyiv, the nation's capital, although they, as well as other respondents, participate in the projects in many parts of the country. Therefore, the study represents initiatives in regeneration of deprived communities and in social entrepreneurship across all Ukraine (Table 6.1).

The Impact of Social Entrepreneurship on Community Development

Three themes important for the development of deprived communities emerged from the interviews:

1. Development of entrepreneurial culture via active citizenship
2. Building entrepreneurial competencies of young people in rural areas
3. Inclusion of disadvantaged individuals in economic activity and fostering their entrepreneurship

Each theme will be discussed in detail.

Development of Entrepreneurial Culture via Active Citizenship

Business venture creation can be approached and supported by a large number of actors using a range of models.

Table 6.1. Interviewees (the Study's Sample).

Participant No.	Gender	Age Group (Years)	Position/Sector	Activity
1	Female	35–39	Lecturer/university	NGO, socially focused projects
2	Male	30–34	Lecturer/university	NGO, socially focused projects
3	Female	20–24	Student/university	NGO, socially focused projects
4	Male	25–29	Entrepreneur/small business owner	Restaurant
5	Female	50–54	Lecturer/university	NGO
6	Female	30–34	Entrepreneur	Training
7	Male	25–30	Entrepreneur/small business owner	Restaurant
8	Male	40–44	Entrepreneur	Online business

9	Male	35–39	Office worker	Social activist
10	Female	30–34	International aid project/member of staff	Social activist
11	Male	30–34	Engineer	NGO, socially focused projects
12	Female	25–29	Office worker/publishing house	Social activist
13	Female	25–29	Local government/member of staff	Local development projects
14	Female	35–39	Local government/member of staff	Local development projects
15	Male	25–29	Entrepreneur/employee of a small business	Coffee shop
16	Male	30–34	Employee of a small business	Restaurant

One of the available approaches is to offer training and skills building that would allow individuals to start their business. Another common approach is to foster ideation about venture creation. This is often accomplished by organising a contest in which participants present their creative ideas and business plans. Globally both approaches are offered by universities, local authorities, international aid organisations, NGOs and businesses and are often free of charge. Many firms also offer professional training for a fee. Due to a large variety of these regularly conducted business training modules, social entrepreneurs seldom offer similar kinds of skill building programmes. However, our study has identified an unusual example of how social entrepreneurship supports venture creation and community development.

Entrepreneurs and NGO activists expressed significant interest toward the comprehensive, multi-dimensional project that is being implemented in Ukraine's city of Ivano-Frankivsk located in Western part of the country, close to the border with Poland, Slovakia, Hungary, Romania and Moldova. Owing to its history (until 1939 the city was part of Poland) and location, Ivano-Frankivsk, a city of more than 230,000 people, enjoys attention and financial support from international donors and investors and is more successful in urban development than many other cities in modern Ukraine. Nonetheless, Ivano-Frankivsk's residents are looking for ways to improve the city's environment and make it even more attractive, exciting and prosperous. In 2014, an entrepreneur in his mid-30s put forward an initiative entitled TownPlus, with an overarching goal to make Ivano-Frankivsk a city that gives its warmth to all its residents and visitors in the form of hospitality, excellent urban facilities and architectural environment, cultural attractions and enticing dining opportunities.[1] The following quote

1 The programme's title has been amended to ensure anonymity.

highlights the participant's excitement with the scope and dimensions of this community development programme:

> *The programme wants to make our city more comfortable for all. The programme wants to transform people's mindset and encourage people to show kindness to each other, hospitality, mutual support. We have deep problems in other parts of the country [i.e. Ukraine] and many people are frustrated and angry. The Ivano-Frankivsk programme is great as it wants to show that things could be different – warm and comfortable for all (Participant 4)*

This is echoed by another participant who notes:

> *Many city governments aim to make their cities beautiful, improve infrastructure, create some things that would be attractive to the visitors. Nothing is wrong with that. It is usually a matter of money and finding investors. But, as a rule, they are not trying to change what people think. In Ivano-Frankivsk the programme leaders took a different approach. They looked at the principal element – that the local community, not just some investors, has to be involved, and this is how people might change their thinking, when they work together for the common good. I think they have already achieved a lot. (Participant 7)*

An essential feature of the broader TownPlus programme is that from the very beginning it has been actively looking to engage businesses in community development. Engaging companies serves the same purpose as engaging citizens – it can be described as collaborative value creation (Berger et al., 2004; Dahan et al., 2010). By the end of 2019, the programme successfully secured participation of 57 business partners.

The TownPlus programme set seven priorities and aims to improve education, urban environment, city governance, ecology, mobility, sports opportunities and entrepreneurship, all with community engagement. The programme leader came up with an idea regarding the principal implementation model. He suggested to launch a restaurant that would generate profit that would become a source of financing for the programme activities. Keeping in mind the need to engage the local community, he put out a call for those who would pay in USD 1,000 each pursuing the goal to attract 100 social activists. The project and the restaurant received the title *FutureCity1* and the required sum has been successfully collected.[2]

The restaurant opened its doors in 2014. It is operated by a restaurant company owned by the entrepreneur who launched the TownPlus programme. The company receives 20% of net profit in return for running the restaurant. The rest of the profit is used for funding socially focused projects. One of the study participants commented on the business model as follows:

> *They identified a very successful model for doing business. This is not a charity as the restaurant works like a normal business – it covers all its expenses, makes profit and keeps part of it. Not all profit, it keeps just 20%. But the operator did not invest anything in this restaurant, other one hundred people did. For the operator there was no investor's risk related to starting any new business. It just used the collected money, rented premises, bought equipment and organised a restaurant. I don't think it was very difficult as the operator runs many other restaurants*

2 The programme's title has been amended to ensure anonymity.

> *and they have very good experience. For those who gave money for this project it was very convenient that some experienced company agreed to take care of business because it simply took all hassle away. (Participant 2)*

Another participant summarised this enterprise's model as follows:

> *It is a win-win format: those who run the restaurant faced no risk, and those who gave money spread risk among themselves, paying in fairly small amount each. The restaurant got additional business, and one hundred socially active people did not want any money in return as they are not investors. All they wanted is a restaurant that works well and makes profit for social projects. (Participant 9)*

As the excerpt correctly indicates, the restaurant founders cannot be viewed as regular investors as they are not looking for investor's gain in the form of profit or other monetary benefits for themselves. They could be called social entrepreneurs: their business makes profit and the larger part of the profit is used for socially orientated projects.

Who are the restaurant founders? Most of them are in their 20s and 30s. They are naturally residents of Ivano-Frankivsk, and they work in a large variety of professions – entrepreneurs, accountants, IT experts, musicians, restaurateurs, staff in finance and banking, and managers in a range of industries.

FutureCity1 positions itself as a community restaurant. In this capacity it became a platform for community gatherings, discussions, games and exhibitions, rather than strictly a place that serves meals and drinks. FutureCity1 invites proposals that would benefit the urban community. The proposals can be submitted any time and are reviewed every week or every other week. They are then reviewed and decisions made by all the founders via an open discussion and voting at FutureCity1. Since its launch, it has held a few hundred events and financially supported dozens of community development projects by giving grants.

Although most grants are small ranging from a few hundred to a few thousand dollars, the grant making activity effectively serves two purposes: community engagement and community development. FutureCity1 supports educational projects, sports events, music festivals, infrastructure development and business start-ups. Many of these projects focus on smaller disadvantaged groups in the city, e.g. students and unemployed women, and, therefore, contribute to alleviation of community problems.

An example of a micro-level initiative supported by a grant from FutureCity1 was a project entitled 'Business Micro Incubator' implemented in 2019 by a social enterprise *HomeForYou*.[3] Using the office space provided by their partner company, HomeForYou organised a working area suitable for short-term work (e.g. a few hours). This area is available for students and mothers who require flexible, rather than fixed, working hours and do not have space or equipment to work at home. To engage with certain business projects or to look for a job they can come to this office, leave their child in the designated play area, and work on the computer provided by HomeForYou with financial support of FutureCity1. HomeForYou does not charge any fees. Although the scope of this project is very small, it offers traditional office environment to those in need and, therefore, facilitates their engagement in economic activity.

Not surprisingly, HomeForYou's collaboration with FutureCity1 has overlapping themes and projects. For

3 The programme's title has been amended to ensure anonymity.

example, HomeForYou offers space for all Ivano-Frankivsk residents to conduct a workshop, give a lecture, offer a MasterClass, organise an exhibition or other event that would promote local crafts or services. In addition, HomeForYou is particularly interested in supporting female entrepreneurship. In 2016–2018, HomeForYou activists offered a series of business-related training sessions for women.

An interviewee offers his assessment of benefits generated by FutureCity1:

> *In many parts of Ukraine, particularly in smaller towns, the situation with availability of jobs is very difficult. FutureCity1 does not create jobs directly by its money, except of the restaurant itself. Rather, by its grants it kick-starts other projects and these projects often transform into entrepreneurial initiatives and create jobs. They may be very small – just one or two people but this is how small businesses are often launched. (Participant 12)*

Another opinion highlights the importance of building community spirit among local residents:

> *They [FutureCity1] are very successful in strengthening the community spirit because people see that they are supported. All projects that they [FutureCity1] finance are published on their Web site, it is totally transparent, and I know that people are encouraged. They see what kinds of projects are funded and they feel that, if they come up with some project, their initiative could be supported too. I know it is important for many. (Participant 14)*

Taken together in a complementary fashion, community spirit strengthening and community development by supporting private initiative that leads to entrepreneurial start-ups and job creation have proven effective (Torri, 2010). Both urban environment and community members draw significant benefits from the social enterprise in the form of FutureCity1.

Over a few years, FutureCity1 became a popular venue among local residents and a must-see tourist place for the city's visitors. Its projects and events are promoted to the community by its own radio station – FutureCity1 Radio – launched in 2015. In addition to playing music, the radio station actively invites speakers, runs talk shows, conducts interviews with prominent people. At a larger scale, the popularity and viability of the concept for social enterprise and community development are further evidenced by more than 200 requests to organise similar enterprises in other countries, i.e. to effectively create a franchise network. FutureCity1 received these requests from Belgium, France, Germany, Ireland, Kazakhstan, Moldova, Russia, the United States and a few cities in Ukraine, which confirms the high impact of the social enterprise platform (Teegen et al., 2004; Pearce and Doh, 2005).

Using the same concept, this innovative model of social entrepreneurship has been successfully implemented in Kyiv, the nation's capital, at a larger scale. The initiative attracted 500 social activists (sometimes called social investors) who paid in USD 1,000 each, and the project received the title 'FutureCityKyiv'.[4] The project established good working relations with a company that designed a restaurant in Kyiv and is managing it. Much like in Ivano-Frankivsk, an operator will be receiving 20% of profit for running a restaurant and the remaining 80% are used for funding, fully or in part, community development projects on a competitive basis. An

4 The programme's title has been amended to ensure anonymity.

NGO that focuses on innovative education and training to unpack individuals' potential played a leading role in launching this project in Kyiv.

Opened in 2018, FutureCityKyiv's restaurant retains most elements of FutureCity1 in Ivano-Frankivsk. In addition to a modern looking, attractively designed restaurant, it serves as a place for meetings, exhibitions, events and all kinds of social interaction. Unlike in Ivano-Frankivsk, FutureCityKyiv more conspicuously emphasises advancement of business ideas and social entrepreneurship for the benefit of the urban community. This is evidenced by its stated goals among which there is an intent to create a transparent fund to finance social projects and start-ups that aim to contribute to the city's development. FutureCityKyiv collects project proposals and applications for funding on an ongoing basis and makes decisions at quarterly general meetings of its members. It also intends to set priorities for future applications, which is an effective tool to focus its funded activities on a certain theme, geographical community within the city, certain disadvantaged group of urban population, launching start-ups and/or development of social entrepreneurship. A study participant commented on this tool:

> *In Ivano-Frankivsk, FutureCity1 wants to do everything to make their city better. They support music festivals, disabled people, school children' activities. It is probably possible and is the right thing to do because their city is small and any promising initiative should be supported. FutureCityKyiv should be more focused as Kyiv is a large city. If they try to support everything and anything, this might look that they entertain themselves rather than focus on urban development. (Participant 15)*

As FutureCityKyiv is fairly new with small experience to date (2019), it remains to be seen what priorities it will be setting, how often they might change and what the ultimate impact on the city's development might be. Furthermore, it might take time for FutureCityKyiv to decide what exactly they want to support, which is a natural process for this kind of engagement with social needs and problems. However, in a large city relying on improvements funded by FutureCityKyiv grants is hardly possible as grant money will never be enough. A more sustainable trajectory is development of entrepreneurial culture and supporting entrepreneurial projects by offering seed funding that would kick-start businesses. The social enterprise's stated goals suggest that FutureCityKyiv intends to do exactly this.

Community Development: The Role of Training People for Volunteer Work

Community development could be approached in a variety of ways. An excellent example is given by the Ukrainian NGO *Poruch* that conducts its activities across the nation. The organisation has an unusual way of mobilising funds for its work. On a regular basis its members donate 10% of their salary to *Poruch* to finance its activity. NGO does not hire any staff and these donations come from the salaries earned elsewhere. In addition, like in many NGOs, members donate their time and do volunteer work.

Poruch implements certain projects funded by the grants from international donors. However, the organisation's principal focus is on training volunteers. From 2015 to 2019 *Poruch* conducted 30 training sessions in many parts of the country. Lasting from two to three days, these sessions are known as the schools for training volunteers. No fewer than

20 trainees participated in each session, and in total more than 750 people have been trained. Training aims to encourage people to become social activists so that they can work as volunteers who would support others. The training sessions build skills of future volunteers, discuss methods of identifying disadvantaged and vulnerable populations in the communities, and highlight ways of including individuals in deprived communities in social interactions and economic activity. Furthermore, *Poruch* aims to engage disadvantaged people as trainees in these sessions and prepare them to do volunteer work for others. The underpinning logic is that encouraging internally displaced persons (IDPs), i.e. those who lost their homes and jobs because of the military conflict with Russia, to actively participate in the life of their hosting communities might significantly foster social cohesion of IDPs and the hosting communities for the common good.

Although training focuses on volunteer work, *Poruch* leaders view this as a critical stepping stone to trainees' engagement in other activities, particularly in social entrepreneurship and/or small business. A study participant explains this:

> *During training people quickly build their confidence that they can do something useful for other people and for themselves. Networking is also an important part of our training. We then help our trainees to get organised, we just tell them what they need get started with a small project. They often ring me afterwards to let me know what they have accomplished and I sense how happy they are! They are typically very grateful that we have introduced them to something new and useful as most of them never thought of becoming a volunteer. (Participant 1)*

Ultimately, these training schools enable people to:

- Identify the needs of disadvantaged populations;
- Identify a range of methods how disadvantaged people could be supported and included in social and economic activity;
- Become active citizens by skill building in how they could engage in volunteer projects and non-for-profit ventures; and
- Establish connections with like-minded people who are interested in volunteer work and social entrepreneurship.

All these objectives have a unifying core in that they aim to make people enterprising and engaged in the life of their communities. Individuals' initiative often begins with identification of opportunity in relation to supporting the disadvantaged, and this gives volunteers a chance for self-fulfilment. Being enterprising also means being resourceful, which are the skills required for both helping the disadvantaged and for entrepreneurship. *Poruch* leaders believe that in certain deprived areas where no jobs are available (e.g. in the communities adjacent to the zone of a military conflict with Russia) the unemployed need to engage in any meaningful activity, and volunteer work gives disadvantaged people this opportunity. Subsequently, volunteer work, via networking and ideation, leads some to greater exposure to employment opportunities and others to entrepreneurship. A study participant describes these links as a snowball effect:

> *They come to our training without any knowledge how they can contribute to community development. We give them this knowledge and connect them with*

> *like-minded people. Of course, we don't expect that they will work as volunteers all their lives. People need to make a living and support their families. After engagement in the community affairs and getting some experience, some volunteers find opportunities to start their own business, others get hired by existing businesses, and I think it is great. We know that later on some of them, hopefully many, will be contributing to their communities again. I have already seen this. (Participant 3)*

The work of NGO *Poruch* can be conceptualised as contribution to revitalising deprived communities by:

- Development of active citizenship;
- Enhancement of support structures for disadvantaged populations by training people, including disadvantaged individuals, for volunteer work in their communities; and
- Widening of job opportunities for volunteers via their engagement in networking and projects with social purpose.

The model formed by NGO *Poruch* – volunteer training plus promotion of active citizenship plus offering networking opportunities – is conceptually robust as its three elements are complementary. Feeding each other, they offer an attractive opportunity for those who are interested in community activism. A logistically weak point is that *Poruch* does not have an unfailing source of revenue to cover its expenses. It depends on the donations of its members, which in the conditions of unstable economy and low incomes is hardly a reliable source of financing. There is little doubt that limited financing sets certain constraints to *Poruch* activities.

Building Entrepreneurial Competencies of Young People in Rural Areas

In 2018–2019, NGO *Poruch* has been implementing another project that contributes to the entrepreneurial culture formation in a more direct way. Funded by an international donor, the project aims to develop entrepreneurial competencies of school children in rural areas. Schools in two rural communities in Ukraine's Kharkiv *oblast* (i.e. a region or province) were chosen for this project, and support of the local authorities was secured from the start. Sixty pupils aged 15 to 19 years were selected and offered training in entrepreneurship and, more generally, in capacity building for active civic engagement. Some examples of the latter were training modules on public speaking, crowdfunding and communication skills.

The training project was initiated in the context of Ukraine's decentralisation processes. In contrast to the previous political structure, local authorities (e.g. a community council, its executive committee and elected council members) now have full responsibility for community affairs and services including education, healthcare, roads, lighting, water provision, waste utilisation, landscaping and safety. Many citizens connect this change with their perception that opportunities (for better services as well as for entrepreneurship) opened up. Although there is less bureaucracy in receiving business licences and permits, launching a business remains challenging for most people, particularly in rural areas, due to lack of everything related to entrepreneurship – from ideation to specific skills to implementation. Critically, entrepreneurial culture in rural areas is missing as residents traditionally were and are engaged in farming.

In this context, training that focuses on the younger segment of population is invaluable as school pupils can be preparing themselves for entrepreneurship early on and ideation begins long before graduation. To this end, *Poruch*, in partnership with the school administration and local authorities, organised a series of training sessions on a range of topics developing knowledge and building skills related to entrepreneurship, leadership, communication, planning and sales. In addition, to ensure sustainability of training modules and enhancement of entrepreneurial culture, *Poruch* trained the local trainers who are able to conduct sessions in the future for other pupils' cohorts. *Poruch* also introduced to the pupils the concept of social entrepreneurship. Furthermore, they created a manual on entrepreneurship for young people living in rural areas. The training programme entitled 'Young Entrepreneurs for Community Growth' was complemented by the strategy for development of entrepreneurship that local authorities in the two communities designed and adopted for 2018–2020.

A study participant made the following comment on the project and its results:

> *During the project, a group of school children launched a small venture – they make shopping bags from ecologically friendly materials. They called them "eco-bags" and started selling them to the supermarkets located in the cities. Isn't it a good result? Of course, their parents helped them. But isn't it great that these pupils show entrepreneurial initiative to their school and the whole community? (Participant 6)*

To summarise, the model designed by NGO *Poruch* includes the following elements:

- Train the trainer programme to ensure sustainability;
- Close collaboration with the local authorities and assisting them to adopt a community-focused strategy for development of entrepreneurship;

- Close collaboration with the school management for mobilising pupils to undertake training;
- Preparation of a manual on entrepreneurship based on the local context;
- Extensive training that included topics beyond entrepreneurship (e.g. leadership, communication);
- Inclusion of the social entrepreneurship concept in entrepreneurship training; and
- Assistance to the trainees to launch a venture.

It is noteworthy that even a very small business venture launched during or as a result of the training programme has symbolic significance showing emergent entrepreneurial culture in a rural community.

Inclusion of Disadvantaged Individuals in Economic Activity and Fostering Their Entrepreneurship

Mission Possible[5]

Effective engagement of disadvantaged people may take various forms. An unusual example is offered in Ukraine by the local community organisation called *Mission Possible* in the city of Poltava. This organisation works with ex-convicts and pursues the goal of integrating them in society by providing employment and the supportive environment for all their living needs. Registered as an NGO, this organisation transformed itself into a social enterprise that has two

5 The organisation's title has been amended to ensure anonymity.

manufacturing facilities, employs staff and earns profit. One facility makes furniture, while the other is a sewing shop.

By operating a small business, *Mission Possible* departs from the charity concept typical for many NGOs and offers a considerably more sustainable model for continuous support of disadvantaged individuals as the established production facilities provide the revenue streams. But how reliable are they? The answer is linked to the entrepreneurial initiative and related skills. The revenue streams will remain reliable as long as the company is able to sell its products. Given the nature of its offering (furniture, clothing, household items such as window curtains etc.), the company is able to stay in business and employ people it wants to support, only by being entrepreneurial and by constantly looking for opportunities to offer new products or models, and to meet customers' demand. Standing still and being complacent with the established production lines leads nowhere; the market may be quickly saturated and the customers may switch to the competitors' products. While it seems that *Mission Possible* does not explicitly train its staff to become entrepreneurs, its business requires an entrepreneurial initiative as all staff are dependent on the company's viability. Therefore, all employees are effectively put in the position where their livelihood depends on their own initiative and skills that would permit to identify new products they can make and sell and, ultimately, make their living.

It is worth noting that, upon receiving certain experience, having built entrepreneurial skills and reestablished links with society, some ex-convicts pursue other options. They find other jobs or launch their own small businesses. There is no doubt that *Mission Possible* not only provides immediate employment opportunities for disadvantaged individuals but also exposes them to the entrepreneurial culture. In these conditions, ideation, business planning, networking and transforming creating thinking into implementation become the natural environment in which individual's engagement with entrepreneurship grows and produces lasting effect for those involved, the community and society at large.

Supporting the Blind

Another example of working with a deprived community is offered by an organisation that supports the blind. This organisation engages the blind in economic activity. About 50% of staff in each of its 79 enterprises are the blind. For example, its branch in the city of Dnipro employs the blind who, under the supervision of managers, make electrical equipment (e.g. electrical switches, plugs etc.) for households and businesses and construction materials. In addition to its sales to large institutional buyers, the company has a retail shop. The volume of the company business is quite impressive. In particular, a branch in Ukraine's city of Bila Tserkva was formed in 1933 and over time grew into one of the principal suppliers of electrical equipment in ex-Soviet space.

Victory-V Group[6]

A vivid – and a very unusual – example of how entrepreneurship could be developed in a deprived community refers to Ukraine's community of veterans. These are mostly young men who participated in an ongoing (in Eastern part of the country) military conflict with breakaway provinces that are sponsored by Russia. Many veterans face significant difficulties reintegrating in society and civic life after their military experience, particularly after they have been in combat. Many develop psychological problems making their adaptation to

6 The organisation's title has been amended to ensure anonymity.

civil life problematic. Owing to these problems, many veterans tend to engage mostly with fellow veterans and rely on them for a range of needs including social interaction, launching a small business, support with getting a job and/or receiving financial help for any kinds of needs. The following example shows how a business – a restaurant called Victory-V – launched by a veteran engages other veterans in the work of this enterprise and offers them opportunities to start their own business via franchise arrangements.

Victory-V restaurant was launched in 2016 in Kyiv by a veteran and his friends. It could be classified as a social enterprise as it uses part of its profits to support fellow veterans and their families. Victory-V swiftly expanded and became a network of companies which included three pizza restaurants in Kyiv, Dnipro and Mariupol, a range of coffee shops in many cities (Kyiv, Mariupol, Kharkiv, Krivoy Rog, among others) and a number of coffee kiosks selling take-away coffee and providing a small seating area (e.g. a small table with a few chairs).

How was Victory-V restaurant launched? Answering this question is critical for understanding the role that the veteran community played in fostering entrepreneurship by its members. Ukraine's veteran network is often viewed as a strongly cohesive closed association of like-minded people. Although the association has its salient disadvantage (i.e. difficulties integrating in the society), it also possesses strong advantages. For example, the veteran network may provide advice for a range of business and personal situations, knowledge sharing, financing for launching a business, support (including financial) and manpower for all kinds of difficult situations in life. The first pizza restaurant was launched by a veteran who from the very beginning consulted with the broader veteran network on most, if not all, issues related to the product line, pricing, service delivery and many other aspects of his business. One of the interviewees commented on the founder's efforts as follows:

> *He did an excellent job talking to all those who were interested in his business idea. Many veterans were excited that their friend was about to launch a pizza restaurant and they offered their opinions on a range of things. It was not an easy task... There were many, in fact too many suggestions. He could not take all of them on board but he was patient enough to explain his views to all. He wanted to hear all kinds of advice, get things right and keep the veterans happy. (Participant 16)*

Rather than entertaining his own ideas about what the pizza restaurant should offer, the founder actively involved many other veterans at all stages of the business and product development. Why was it necessary? Another interviewee argued that the restaurant founder is not risk-averse; he is willing to take calculated risk as most entrepreneurs.

> *Of course, there was risk involved in launching this business. You never know whether customers would like to buy your product, how they perceive the prices and if they find a restaurant attractive. But he wanted to minimise risk and that's why he wanted to understand how the veterans perceive his future business. Some people gave good advice, other didn't, but it was important to seek advice from all. (Participant 7)*

Risk minimisation and crowdsourcing to shape the future restaurant's business model were the two interlinked reasons for seeking extensive advice from the veteran association (Lang et al., 2016). The opinions were sought from not a defined group but rather an evolving cohort, with the purpose to discuss ideas, receive ideas and seek feedback. Effectively, the restaurant founder used social product development (SPD) and open innovation at all stages of launching his business including opportunity identification, ideation and concepting (Schaefer, 2014; Evans et al., 2015; Forbes and Schaefer, 2017).

The SPD benefits can be summarised as follows:

- Continuous product development was achieved by involving veterans in all stages of business design.
- The costs of developing a business model and relevant products were significantly reduced by consulting with veterans, rather than professional managers, marketing and logistics experts.
- Risk of unsuccessful launch was mitigated by securing informal approval of the business model by the broader veteran network.
- As many current customers are veterans who naturally, due to their feeling of belonging to the network, make comments and suggestions regarding all aspects of the pizza restaurant, this allowed to incorporate customers in the business development process (Peterson and Schaefer, 2014).

It is unsurprising that Victory-V restaurant served as a business appealing to fellow veterans for replication. Once this model was used by other veterans, accompanied by the launch of many coffee shops and kiosks carrying the Victory-V brand, the Victory-V Group was formed. The Group became a franchise in which all pizza restaurants, coffee shops and kiosks are owned individually. The leader of this franchise network – a veteran who launched the first pizza restaurant – set the rule that owners of the pizza restaurants and coffee shops and kiosks must be veterans, rather than entrepreneurs from the general public, and that each franchisee pays 5% of profit to the parent company (i.e. the first Victory-V restaurant). The franchise leader earmarks this money for veterans' support, which goes towards assisting families of those who became disabled or lost lives as a result of a military conflict.

Support of veterans' families, which is built in the business model, raises the question about the nature of this business. Should it be categorised as social entrepreneurship? The study participants who are well aware of Victory-V operations overwhelmingly asserted that the restaurant owner does not view his business as a social enterprise and persistently avoids using this concept and terminology. Rather, he argues that it is a normal business pursuing the goal of making profit. His employees confirmed that, other things equal, he would prefer to hire veterans but his preference is constrained by other, more important business-related goals, particularly by the need to get things done. An interviewee provided the following comment:

> *The restaurant is a business, and we are in business for profit. We want to hire veterans because we view ourselves as part of the veteran community. But a candidate [a veteran] needs to be suitable for the job. We don't hire people just because they are veterans and need a job. (Participant 15)*

Although the restaurant owner is a veteran himself and is very interested in supporting the bonds with other individuals with military experience, he has taken a pragmatic stance viewing the sustainability of his business as a top priority, rather than labelling his company as a social enterprise.

Nonetheless, the owner has made a salient contribution to developing entrepreneurship in and for disadvantaged community of veterans:

- Together with his associates, he effectively utilised the veteran community as an entrepreneurial ecosystem (Leenders and Dolfsma, 2016). Although this was not the first case of using the veteran network for business creation, Victory-V was an example of a large-scale and extremely successful engagement of the network resources. For other community members, this is a powerful success story that they may wish to repeat.
- Victory-V has developed a business model that has already been and is being replicated by fellow veterans. The model rests on the use of veteran community resources, engages veterans as co-creators (via open innovation) and customers, includes some features of a social enterprise and is truly replicable.
- The Victory-V brand and underpinning models created a range of entrepreneurial opportunities for other community members. Many businesses within the Group, particularly coffee shops and kiosks, require small investment, which gives opportunities to launch a business to a broad spectrum of veterans, with varying interest, financial and administrative resources.

CONCLUSION

As the military conflict between Ukraine's central government and the breakaway regions continues, more and more veterans join the network and it keeps growing fast. Unfortunately, this deprived community will exist for a long time until each member fully integrates in society, although it is likely to be extremely challenging to those with disabilities.

The entrepreneurship model for the deprived community of veterans was developed by the deprived community itself. The framework for this development was open innovation in which ideas, products and delivery methods were sourced from many parties, rather than done in-house. However, the veteran-entrepreneurs engaged exclusively members of the veteran community and did not cross its boundaries to ensure full-scale SPD. This is because veterans strictly adhere to their own values, but not other people. Regardless of the restrictions placed on open innovation, the veterans successfully created a range of entrepreneurial opportunities from which many in the veteran community may benefit.

The veterans' experience is different from efforts to develop a deprived community by projects like FutureCity1 and FutureCityKyiv. In those projects, so-called social investors lead the activities. Their investment (USD 1,000) is not an investment in the traditional meaning as they do not expect any monetary return and will never receive their money back. Rather, their investment is an indication of their strong interest in community regeneration. The collective contribution of 100 and 500 people, respectively, formed the platform for community development activities including social entrepreneurship. In all examples discussed in this chapter – the FutureCity projects and veteran businesses – enhancement of entrepreneurial culture in the communities is a notable core.

LEARNING POINTS

- Engagement of NGO activists, social entrepreneurs, companies and local governments in collaborative value creation is a promising way of mobilising local resources for the revitalisation of deprived communities. It is worth emphasising the collaborative nature of work as a growing trend and a requirement of today for achieving the best results.

- As social entrepreneurs are particularly creative in finding innovative methods for attracting citizens to make social investment (i.e. to pay in money without expecting financial gains for themselves), their ability to raise funds and add own effort to address the needs of disadvantaged populations and/or deprived neighbourhoods should be fully used and further enhanced. Local governments could achieve this by partnering with socially focused ventures and offering them support, e.g. by leasing unused or abandoned buildings and plots for a long term at no cost or for a nominal fee, and/or sponsoring events and activities aimed at improvements in the locality.
- Ideation by social entrepreneurs is a critical element that might have an enormous positive impact on deprived communities. Social entrepreneurs realise this by their grant-making activity, supporting mostly small-scale projects and giving aspiring entrepreneurs a chance to build skills, acquire confidence in their abilities and make a change in the community and the lives of disadvantaged groups.
- Capacity building activities by social entrepreneurs could be a powerful tool for fostering entrepreneurship in a range of communities, e.g. in rural areas by training school children in the fundamentals of entrepreneurship. Similar training for creating and running a small venture might be useful in many localities, deprived by the lack of employment opportunities, and for many disadvantaged populations, e.g. mothers who do not have space and possibilities to

work from home. Local and regional governments might partner with entrepreneurs and social entrepreneurs to offer this training on a regular basis.

- Training specifically in social entrepreneurship is an innovative way of engaging people in community activism for the benefit of deprived communities.

REFERENCES

Austin, J., Stevenson, H. and Wei-Skillern, J. 2006. Social and commercial entrepreneurship: same, different, or both? *Entrepreneurship: Theory and Practice*, 30, 1–22.

Bacq, S. and Janssen, F. 2011. The multiple faces of social entrepreneurship: a review of definitional issues based on geographical and thematic criteria, *Entrepreneurship & Regional Development*, 23(5–6), 373–403.

Berger, I.E., Cunningham, P.H. and Drumwright, M.E. 2004. Social alliances: company/nonprofit collaboration, *California Management Review*, 47(1), 58–90.

Certo, S.T. and Miller, T. 2008. Social entrepreneurship: key issues and concepts, *Business Horizons*, 51(4), 267–271.

Choi, N. and Majumdar, S. 2014. Social entrepreneurship as an essentially contested concept: opening a new avenue for systematic future research, *Journal of Business Venturing*, 29(3), 363–376.

Dahan, N.M., Doh, J.P., Oetzel, J. and Yaziji, M. 2010. Corporate-NGO collaboration: co-creating new business models for developing markets, *Long Range Planning*, 43(2–3), 326–342.

Evans, R.D., Gao, J.X., Martin, N. and Simmonds, C. 2015. Integrating social knowledge and collaboration tools into dispersed product development, *International Journal of Advanced Corporate Learning*, 8(2), 20–27.

Forbes, H. and Schaefer, D. 2017. Social product development: the democratization of design, manufacture and innovation, *Procedia CIRP*, 60, 404–409.

International Monetary Fund 2019. *World Economic Outlook Database*, April 2019. Available at: https://www.imf.org/external/pubs/ft/weo/2019/01/weodata/weorept.aspx?sy=2017&ey=2024&ssd=1&sort=country&ds=.&br=1&pr1.x=55&pr1.y=10&c=921%2C926&s=NGDPDPC&grp=0&a=

Janssen, F., Fayolle, A. and Wuilaume, A. 2018. Researching bricolage in social entrepreneurship, *Entrepreneurship & Regional Development*, 30(3–4), 450–470.

Lang, M., Bharadwaj, N. and Di Benedetto, C.A. 2016. How crowdsourcing improves prediction of market-oriented outcomes, *Journal of Business Research*, 69(10), 4168–4176.

Leenders, R.T.A.J. and Dolfsma, W.A. 2016. Social networks for innovation and new product development, *Journal of Product Innovation Management*, 33(2), 123–131.

Lyon, F. and Sepulveda, L. 2009. Mapping social enterprises: past approaches, challenges and future directions, *Social Enterprise Journal*, 5(1), 83–94.

Moss, T.W., Short, J.C., Payne, G.T. and Lumpkin, G.T. 2011. Dual identities in social ventures: an exploratory study, *Entrepreneurship: Theory and Practice*, 35(4), 805–830.

Mouraviev, N. and Koulouri, A. Eds 2019. *Energy Security: Policy Challenges and Solutions for Resource Efficiency*, London, Palgrave Macmillan.

Pearce, J.A. and Doh, J.P. 2005. The high impact of collaborative social initiatives, *Sloan Management Review*, 46(2), 30–39.

Peterson, A.K. and Schaefer, D. 2014. Social product development: introduction, overview, and current status. In *Product Development in the Socio-Sphere: Game Changing Paradigms for 21st Century Breakthrough Product Development and Innovation*, Eds D. Schaefer, pp. 1–33, New York, NY, Springer.

Schaefer, D. Ed. 2014. *Product Development in the Socio-Sphere: Game Changing Paradigms for 21st Century Breakthrough Product Development and Innovation*, New York, NY, Springer.

Teegen, H., Doh, J.P. and Vachani, S. 2004. The importance of nongovernmental organizations (NGOs) in global governance and value creation: an international business research agenda, *Journal of International Business Studies*, 35(6), 463–483.

The Heritage Foundation 2019. *The 2019 Index of Economic Freedom*. Available at: www.heritage.org

Torri, M. 2010. Community-based enterprises: a promising basis towards an alternative entrepreneurial model for sustainability enhancing livelihoods and promoting socio-economic development in rural India, *Journal of Small Business and Entrepreneurship*, 23(2), 237–248.

7

LIFESTYLE ENTREPRENEURS: UNPACKING THEIR POTENTIAL FOR DEPRIVED COMMUNITIES

INTRODUCTION

The term 'lifestyle entrepreneur' refers to those entrepreneurs who are focused on maintaining a certain way of life and whose 'business success might best be measured in terms of a continuing ability to perpetuate their chosen lifestyle' (Dewhurst and Horobin, 1998, p. 30). The business philosophy of lifestyle entrepreneurs contrasts with common business practice centred on business growth and development. Some scholars (Dewhurst and Horobin, 1998; Shaw and Williams, 2004; McGinn, 2005) argue that such a non-economic business philosophy creates problems for economic growth in a region or a country in general. However, if a lifestyle entrepreneur is situated in a deprived community her/his enterprising efforts are arguably in sync with the values and economic profile of the chosen locality.

Entrepreneurship in general is a thought-provoking, bewildering concept. Past and current entrepreneurship research has been devoted to understanding what successful entrepreneurs have done, what could be done by entrepreneur-aspirants, and what kind of business failures could be avoided. However, there is a lack of a universally accepted definition of entrepreneurship. Some refer to entrepreneurship as new venture creation (Low and MacMillan, 1988; Brush and Chaganti, 1996; Fletcher and Harris, 2002), while others equate entrepreneurship with running small- or medium-sized enterprises (Anderson and McAuley, 1999; Macrì et al., 2002). Casson (2003) disagrees with equating entrepreneurship exclusively with ownership and claims that an entrepreneur is a person who specialises in making 'judgemental decisions about the coordination of scarce resources' (Casson, 2003, p. 20). For Casson, entrepreneurs are experts who use their judgement to deal with complex problems and allocation of scarce resources in the conditions characterised by uncertainty and risk. This definition applies to lifestyle entrepreneurs operating in deprived areas.

WHO IS A LIFESTYLE ENTREPRENEUR?

The term 'lifestyle entrepreneur' tends to imply that 'lifestyle' and 'entrepreneur' are two distinct spheres. While *lifestyle* is implicitly related to low tolerance of work effort, *entrepreneur* is typically associated with hard work and a profit-oriented drive. Lifestyle entrepreneurs could be defined as those entrepreneurs who do business with less emphasis on monetary rewards. In other words, monetary rewards are not a priority. There are three main characteristics of lifestyle entrepreneurs: first, they align entrepreneurial activity with their preferred lifestyle (Ateljevic and Doorne, 2000; McGinn, 2005; Milanesi, 2018); second, they prioritise their personal goals that are often in sync with the values of the chosen locality over business objectives (Bolton and Thompson, 2003; McGinn, 2005; Milanesi, 2018); and finally, they are not growth oriented (Ateljevic and Doorne, 2000; Burns, 2001; Claire, 2012).

Lifestyle entrepreneurs tend to utilise fewer resources, employ fewer people and thus inherently constrain their own growth and ultimately also local and/or regional economic development, hence having a direct impact on area's deprivation index measured by the Office for National Statistics in the United Kingdom (McGinn, 2005). Lifestyle entrepreneurs lack entrepreneurial ambitions for business expansion; their business objectives are secondary to their personal goals (Milanesi, 2018). They are willing to reject business opportunities in order to 'preserve their quality of life in their socio-environmental contexts' (Ateljevic and Doorne, 2000, p. 388). For that reason, some researchers suggest that the success of lifestyle entrepreneurs can be best measured in terms of their ability to maintain their chosen lifestyle rather than financial success (Dewhurst and Horobin, 1998; Ateljevic and Doorne, 2000; Claire, 2012; Milanesi, 2018).

Lifestyle entrepreneurs tend to choose a lifestyle-oriented venture rather than a profit maximising one. They choose to maintain a certain lifestyle and thus they tend to be satisfied with that instead of pursuing innovation in their ventures. As such, lifestyle entrepreneurs have distinctive goals centred on their style of living while employing rather minimalistic business operation methods, compared to their growth-oriented counterparts in the same sectors (Shaw and Williams, 2004). This view is supported by McClelland's theory of needs, which suggests that every individual has a different balance of three essential needs: power, achievement and affiliation (McClelland, 1987). People with different priorities and goals have different sets of strategies for running their business.

Work motivation literature sheds further light on the work attitudes of lifestyle entrepreneurs. Maslow's hierarchy of needs suggests that physiological needs must be met prior to other needs, such as social needs and self-actualisation needs (Maslow, 1943). However, this is not observed in the case of lifestyle entrepreneurs since they aim to satisfy these needs simultaneously rather than independently. People are different and thus their needs vary. Expectancy theory puts forward the idea that 'people have preferences among outcomes' (Vroom, 2005, p. 239). Vroom (2005) argues that individuals critically weigh up and select working behaviour that would result in the best rewarding outcomes from their perspective. In the case of lifestyle entrepreneurs, they take calculated risks for creating and running a venture in exchange of pursuit of their preferred lifestyle. In a study of micro-businesses, the owners who have no growth intention appear to understand the potential dangers and instability of business expansion (Greenbank, 2001), supporting Vroom's (2005) claim that individuals critically assess risks before making behavioural choices.

Another perspective is offered by goal-setting theory suggesting that easily attained goals tend to result in lower performance than specific and higher-level goals (Locke and Latham, 2006). For lifestyle entrepreneurs, their major concern is business survival, which leads McGinn (2005) to argue that such easily attained goals are a constraint to business growth and economic development in general. McGinn's view is supported by empirical studies (e.g. Smallbone et al., 1995; Gray, 2006) that report that a growth intent is positively related to organisational performance. However, there has been a lack of longitudinal studies showing whether or not growth aspirations are being realised.

Other scholars argue that lifestyle entrepreneurs may turn their ventures into high-growth ventures, which eventually contributes to economic development at the local, reginal and national levels. Although lifestyle ventures are not growth oriented in their essence, it is not uncommon for them to grow into larger ventures. One notable lifestyle entrepreneur, who turned into high-growth entrepreneur, is Ewing Marion Kauffman. Despite Kauffman's original intent described as 'just making a living' (Rogers and Makonnen, 2002, p. 3), his business ultimately generated over USD 5 million in annual revenues by 1986. A survey conducted by *Inc.* magazine reveals that 48% of the 500 fastest-growing companies in the United States are indeed run by lifestyle entrepreneurs. According to the survey, 35% of 500 companies aimed for slow or slower growth, while 13% of the companies originally chose not to grow at all (Hyatt and Mamis, 1997). This study not only contradicts scholarly views (Smallbone et al., 1995; McGinn, 2005; Gray, 2006) but also reveals that lifestyle entrepreneurs are not detrimental to economic development despite profit-making not being their top priority.

This orientation of lifestyle entrepreneurs does not adequately reflect their potential and ability. In a study of lifestyle ventures, strategic capabilities were found to correlate positively with business performance (Lerner and Almor, 2002). This study implies that lifestyle entrepreneurs possess the potential and ability to grow, despite the fact that initially they have no intention to grow. The rejection of profit orientation as a business philosophy is not totally harmful for a small enterprise and its development. Based on a seven-year-long case study in New Zealand, Ateljevic and Doorne (2000) concluded that lifestyle and non-economic motives provide sufficient stimuli for the growth of small businesses, which is in contrast to McGinn's (2005) argument that the lifestyle orientation could result in the stagnation of an enterprise.

Lifestyle entrepreneurs not only seek business survival to make a living, they also seek autonomy, well-being and the enjoyment of work. They assess their risks and outcomes critically before starting a new venture and put in a lower level of work effort in order to satisfy their needs concurrently rather than consecutively. Although lifestyle entrepreneurs have little or no intention to grow, this does not necessarily mean that lifestyle entrepreneurs are not capable of ensuring business growth. An intention to grow is not a sufficient condition for business growth since intention does not represent capability. For the firms lacking an entrepreneurial capability it is difficult to grow, although these firms have high-growth objectives. Furthermore, non-financial orientation is not about money aversion. Lifestyle and non-economic motives can also lead to financial success and economic growth (Ateljevic and Doorne, 2000).

INTRINSIC MOTIVATION: FOCUS ON A SENSE OF ACCOMPLISHMENT AND PERSONAL SATISFACTION

As with other categories of entrepreneurs, lifestyle entrepreneurs aim to create and run their own ventures, often with minimal effort. Despite their determination and capacity to take calculated risks, they tend to follow a radically different business philosophy and/or orientation. Most of the literature highlights the entrepreneur's motivation in establishing a new venture. Scholars suggest that entrepreneurs are driven by a combination of intrinsic (Smith and Miner, 1983; Segal et al., 2005; Yang, 2007; Kuratko, 2008) and monetary rewards (Swedberg, 2000; Segal et al., 2005; Yang, 2007). However, lifestyle entrepreneurs have a greater focus on intrinsic aspects than monetary incentives, while the latter are viewed as a means to an end, associated with financial independence in order to support a certain lifestyle. This tendency to favour a chosen lifestyle over other possible motives for establishing an enterprise shapes the lifestyle entrepreneur's mindset towards opportunity recognition, business growth and innovation.

Guercinia and Cova (2018) consider the lifestyle entrepreneur as one of the representative types of unconventional entrepreneurs. For lifestyle entrepreneurs, profits may not represent a source of fuel for business growth; rather, profits may stand for a source of security for them to continue their desired lifestyle (Glancey, 1998). Monetary rewards become second priority in comparison to desired lifestyle and personal satisfaction. They enjoy the act of engaging in a business and being appreciated by consumers at the same time, which gives lifestyle entrepreneurs a sense of accomplishment and personal satisfaction (Dominici et al., 2019). To sum up, work–life balance, flexible working, living in a preferred location and also the opportunity to generate income from a hobby or desired lifestyle experience are key characteristics of lifestyle entrepreneurs.

The fundamental feature that distinguishes lifestyle entrepreneurship from mainstream entrepreneurship is the intent to grow. Unlike entrepreneurs who are eager to expand their ventures, lifestyle entrepreneurs put emphasis on personal, non-financial goals. In relation to that, lifestyle entrepreneurs are willing to sacrifice business-centred aspirations in exchange for low work effort and a less stressful working life (Carson et al., 2018). Since lifestyle entrepreneurs prioritise quality of life and social value, they are unenthusiastic about business growth. Table 7.1 summarises the differences between lifestyle and mainstream entrepreneurs.

The differences between lifestyle and mainstream entrepreneurs are more apparent in terms of operational activities. It is very unlikely that lifestyle entrepreneurs would increase or optimise units of production since this approach would complicate business operations, not to mention the burden of possible additional capital investment. However, intention to grow cannot be equated to capability to grow.

Table 7.1. Differences between Lifestyle Entrepreneurs and Other Entrepreneurs.

	Lifestyle Entrepreneurs	Entrepreneurs
Impression	Lifestyle entrepreneurs are less committed to business growth	Entrepreneurs are more profit-oriented and committed to business growth
Business philosophy	Business aspiration is typically sacrificed	Profit-maximisation
Orientation	Work–life balance Quality of life Personal satisfaction	Economic value
Process	Flexible work schedule	24/7 work-centred lifestyle

Despite the impression that lifestyle entrepreneurs are not devoted to business growth and expansion, this does not imply that they cannot grow their ventures into large firms. In some cases, lifestyle entrepreneurs even commit to innovate without jeopardising their modest business objectives (Dominici et al., 2019). However, lifestyle orientation may become less important over time (Mottiar, 2007) and some lifestyle entrepreneurs move beyond a lifestyle venture to a growth-focused venture (Attree et al., 2018). It thus appears that defining lifestyle entrepreneurship solely on the basis of the lifestyle motive is somewhat problematic.

KEY STUDIES IN THE FIELD OF LIFESTYLE ENTREPRENEURSHIP

Most empirical studies of lifestyle entrepreneurs explore their motivation and the socio-economical implications of their activities at the regional or national levels. For example, Ateljevic and Doorne (2000) suggest that lifestyle entrepreneurs play a critical role in stimulating economic growth and regional development. Citing the Waitomo region in New Zealand as an example, Ateljevic and Doorne (2000) reported that lifestyle entrepreneurs attract profit-oriented entrepreneurs to exploit market opportunities and promote regional development. Others, such as Carson et al. (2018), examined the urban–rural migration of lifestyle entrepreneurs in Northern Sweden and concluded that the niche-oriented business models fill market gaps that were not taken up by local entrepreneurs. However, Carson et al. (2018) also questioned the longevity of the development brought by lifestyle-oriented migrants because lifestyle entrepreneurs may relocate in search of their preferred settings. Consistent with the argument of Carson et al. (2018), Sun and Xu (2017) argued that lifestyle entrepreneurs are highly mobile and ready to relocate multiple times. Moreover, outsiders often have an idealised image of countryside or rural living and thus conflict may arise between newcomers and the traditional local population over the use of resources and income generation activities (Jæger, 2020). For outsiders, the countryside is more about leisure activities and counter-urban living (Carson et al., 2018), whereas traditional local residents consider agricultural production as their main focus. In recent years, however, the combination of hospitality with guided farm tours is increasingly popular, fuelling the rise of agrotourism (also called agritourism) (Dominici et al., 2019).

A brief review of the literature published in peer-reviewed journals in the past 20 years allows to argue that the extant lifestyle entrepreneurship research is far from being conclusive on motivation, aspiration and business trajectory of lifestyle entrepreneurs, which Table 7.2 shows.

One of the earliest studies using the term 'lifestyle entrepreneur' is the study of Ateljevic and Doorne (2000), which described the rise of entrepreneurially minded individuals who developed product and services within a distinctive lifestyle

Table 7.2. Summary of Key Studies in Lifestyle Entrepreneurship.

Author	Method	Sector	Sample Size	Country of Study
Dahles and Bras (1999)	Anthropological fieldwork; interview	Tourism	100	Indonesia
Ateljevic and Doorne (2000)	Case study; interview; focus group; observation	Tourism	150	New Zealand
Shaw and Williams (2004)	Interview	Tourism	6	United Kingdom
Mottiar (2007)	Interview	Tourism	10	Ireland
Lashley and Rowson (2010)	Survey	Tourism	127	United Kingdom
Marchant and Mottiar (2011)	Case study; interview	Sport; surfing	6	Ireland
Skokic and Morrison (2011)	Interview	Tourism	33	Croatia
Claire (2012)	Survey	No mention	154	United States
Xu and Feng (2015)	Case study; interview; observation	Food	3	China

Table 7.2. (*Continued*)

Author	Method	Sector	Sample Size	Country of Study
Sun and Xu (2017)	Case study; interview	Tourism	30	China
Carson et al. (2018)	Interview	Tourism	15	Sweden
Attree et al. (2018)	Case study	Artisan; honey-making	1	Australia
Dominici et al. (2019)	Interview	Artisan; wine-making	10	Italy

framework. Lifestyle reflects personal beliefs and attitudes towards work, leisure, people and the environment. A lifestyle venture is thus a business that attempts to encompass a particular way of living, interests or attitudes as a unique selling point. With increased commercialisation and imitation by competitors over time, Ateljevic and Doorne (2000) demonstrated how lifestyle entrepreneurship creates a new niche market which consequently results in a high level of market segmentation and service differentiation.

Dahles and Bras (1999) described romantic tourism in Indonesia in late 1990s where entrepreneurial-minded local street guides sell a variety of goods and services, including their way of living. For that reason, the study of Dahles and Bras (1999) is included in this review despite the authors did not explicitly use the term 'lifestyle entrepreneurs'.

To a great extent, the business environment determines the level of innovativeness and competitiveness of all entrepreneurs including lifestyle entrepreneurs. Most studies on lifestyle entrepreneurship are conducted in the context of developed countries, such as the United Kingdom and the United States. The type of business associated with lifestyle entrepreneurs is closely linked to the cultural context and business environment they operate in. The study of Dominici et al. (2019) revolves around lifestyle entrepreneurs operating in the wine-making sector in the context of rural Italy. Some of the interviewed participants run family businesses and were open to the idea of expanding their family trade. This indicates one distinctive characteristic of lifestyle entrepreneurs: the intimate family vibe. Most lifestyle entrepreneurs pursue their objectives by adopting a form of partnership among family members and spouses (Sun and Xu, 2017; Attree et al., 2018; Carson et al., 2018). This characteristic is further emphasised with those businesses where the extended family lives on the same premises as guests (Lashley and Rowson, 2010).

Another distinctive characteristic of lifestyle entrepreneurship is its tendency to stay small size and avoid subsequent reinvestment. The decision not to expand a business is often associated with a desire to retain control over decision-making (Glancey, 1998) alongside financial constraints (Attree et al., 2018). Naturally, many lifestyle entrepreneurs prefer not to expand their businesses in order to maintain the established and desired lifestyle (Carson et al., 2018), which, however, is subject to change in line with evolving motivation (Marchant and Mottiar, 2011).

A study of lifestyle entrepreneurs in Croatia provides an insight into a transition economy which was not originally supportive of entrepreneurship (Skokic and Morrison, 2011). Unlike the Italians, the Croatians reject family employment and prefer hiring qualified personnel. More importantly, Skokic and Morrison (2011) argue that the concept of lifestyle entrepreneurship is derived in the context of the Western economy which overlooks the existence of diverse world-views. Likewise, Sun and Xu (2017) reported a different concept of lifestyle in China, where Chinese lifestyle entrepreneurs prepare to return eventually to where they came from and consider lifestyle ventures as a temporary escape from urban living.

Xu and Feng (2015) studied the home restaurant sector in China in which diners can enjoy home-style cooking. They identified that Chinese lifestyle entrepreneurs in this sector found a niche demand for home cooking in non-commercialised settings. Typically, they offer home-style meals and cooking services in their homes or in residential dwellings, characterised by a careful selection of ingredients to meet diners' expectations of taste amplified by the warmth and care associated with a home-made meal. For them, home restaurants are created rather for social purposes than purely monetary gains. Consistent with other studies (e.g. Carson et al., 2018), lifestyle entrepreneurs in China prefer to stay small and control the size of their operations to maintain the family distinctive ambience (Xu and Feng, 2015).

The study of Xu and Feng (2015) not only indicates a new pattern of consumption but also emphasises a relational aspect of lifestyle entrepreneurship. The process of creating a relaxing atmosphere, establishing emotional attachment and providing home-cooked meals gives the service provider an experience similar to that of the consumer. Such blurred distinctions between production and consumption redefine value creation because both consumer and producer participate in the process of value creation and consumption. The personal values of lifestyle entrepreneurs in this case emerge as shared values and are subsequently translated into economic benefit (Cederholm and Hultman, 2010). Carson et al. (2018) noted that some lifestyle entrepreneurs carefully avoid operations that do not match their ethical values and focus on catering to the needs of customers who share the same personal values. The rejection of business expansion and careful selection of clientele indicate a high level of service differentiation (Cederholm and Hultman, 2010), which may lead the service provider to become a market leader in the long run.

Studies of lifestyle entrepreneurship also observed a range of entrepreneurial cultures, including cultures both supportive and unsupportive of entrepreneurship. Entrepreneurial culture often stems from the Western economic system, although a few studies explore lifestyle entrepreneurship in transition economies (e.g. Skokic and Morrison, 2011; Sun and Xu, 2017). Skokic and Morrison (2011) reported the non-existence of lifestyle entrepreneurship in Croatia and argued that the traditional view of lifestyle entrepreneurship is not applicable in the context of Croatia and its transition economy in general. Mainly, this is due to the strong influence of socialist views, corruption, restriction of private economic activities and the subsequent negative attitudes towards entrepreneurship in this country (Skokic and Morrison, 2011). Lifestyle entrepreneurship in China, on the other hand, shares similar characteristics with European lifestyle entrepreneurship, namely family involvement in operations (Xu and Feng, 2015), emphasis on the quality of life (Xu and Feng, 2015; Sun and Xu, 2017) and escape from urban living (Sun and Xu, 2017).

Many lifestyle entrepreneurs engage in tourism (Ateljevic and Doorne, 2000; Mottiar, 2007; Claire, 2012; Carson et al., 2018) and artisan industries (Attree et al., 2018; Dominici et al., 2019). Scholarly views regarding the skill set of lifestyle entrepreneurs are mixed. The artisan sector is seen as involving highly skilled craftsmanship and requires entrepreneurial passion to turn a hobby into a feasible business. The tourism industry, on the other hand, attracts lifestyle entrepreneurs because of low legal and professional barriers to entry (Lashley and Rowson, 2010). In a sample of nearly 130 hoteliers in the United Kingdom, Lashley and Rowson (2010) found that lifestyle entrepreneurs lack the necessary know-how to manage a leisure and hospitality business. In contrast, Marchant and Mottiar (2011) claimed that lifestyle entrepreneurs in Ireland are well educated and characterised by business acumen. Researchers reported that lifestyle entrepreneurs tend to migrate and establish their new venture in rural or peripheral areas, citing escaping stressful urban life as a push factor and local environment as a pull factor (Sun and Xu, 2017; Carson et al., 2018). This finding indicates the dominance of a desired lifestyle as a leitmotif with an almost inevitable change of priorities over time.

Claire (2012, p. 37) pointed out that a change in the perception of the 'entrepreneurial ideal' may occur due to the retirement of baby boomers and rise of Generation Y. Generational differences in terms of values and personal goals are especially noteworthy. The younger generation values work–life balance and a meaningful job, which is congruent with the ambitions of the majority of lifestyle entrepreneurs. Moreover, millennials are digital natives and tend to heavily rely on digital devices for daily activities, including financial transactions and communication. This indicates not only a key difference between older and younger generation, but also the main characteristic of the digital lifestyle: staying connected with the global virtual audience.

CHANGES IN LIFESTYLE ENTREPRENEURSHIP IN THE DIGITAL AGE

Increased global connectivity facilitates the rise of influencing marketeers and the sharing economy. Entrepreneurship researchers observed a new mode of consumption in which consumers play an active role (Milanesi, 2018). The growing trend to 'commercialise emotional bonds' (Guercinia and Cova, 2018, p. 388) points to the significant role of community arrangements in the digital age. The passion for sharing with other internet users not only 'drives consumption', but also 'generates new forms of entrepreneurship' (Milanesi, 2018, p. 425). Although the phenomenon of networking with consumers is not new, technological innovations in this field simplify the networking process and optimise financial outcomes. The growth of ridesharing firms, such as Uber, and home-sharing services, such as AirBnB, indicates the emergence of 'collaborative lifestyle' that combines 'the benefits of ownership with reduced personal burden and cost' and also lowers environmental impact (Botsman and Rogers, 2010, p. 10). Central to the development of the sharing economy is the use of technology and collaborative consumption, thereby allowing lifestyle-oriented individuals to take advantage of low-cost entry to serve market demand. It is worth emphasising that online platforms, such as Uber and AirBnB, facilitate flexible work arrangements that give individuals opportunities to enter a much wider market than traditional physical platforms, with relatively low costs and low risk.

The 'collaborative lifestyle' phenomenon changes the perception of how entrepreneurs identify and exploit market opportunities in the sharing economy. They have little or no genuine interest in the product or service they provide. Participating in online platforms (e.g. ridesharing and home sharing) provides them with financial independence, spatial flexibility and the possibility of higher earnings than conventional day jobs offer.

Previous research has tended to classify lifestyle entrepreneurship based on motivation (Shaw and Williams, 2004; Bredvold and Skålén, 2016; Carson et al., 2018). Owing to this, characteristics, such as entrepreneurial passion and market size, have been often ignored by previous research. As earlier studies concluded, lifestyle entrepreneurs are not a homogeneous group. They work according to varying degrees of desired lifestyle and economic motives (Marchant and Mottiar, 2011; Bredvold and Skålén, 2016; Carson et al., 2018). Lifestyle entrepreneurship may therefore comprise an entrepreneurial continuum with quite diverse personal and business goals. The range of lifestyle entrepreneurs includes: a pure lifestyle seeker, who solely considers lifestyle ideals and lacks ambition for long-term development (Lashley and Rowson, 2010; Sun and Xu, 2017); lifestyle opportunist who capitalises on a lifestyle market with little or no genuine interest in the product or service itself (Skokic and Morrison, 2011); loyal lifestyle entrepreneur who identifies a niche market and stays small to serve like-minded customers (Cederholm and Hultman, 2010; Xu and Feng, 2015; Carson et al., 2018); and tribal lifestyle entrepreneurship that is supported by a community of enthusiasts who in turn reinforce the entrepreneur's passion for the product or service (Guercinia and Cova, 2018). Fig. 7.1 summarises the types of lifestyle entrepreneurs in the context of their passion and the market size they serve.

Tribal lifestyle entrepreneurship is notably under-represented among lifestyle entrepreneurs because this type of entrepreneurship has been traditionally associated with an

	Low passion	High passion
High volume	Lifestyle opportunist	Tribal lifestyle entrepreneurship
Low volume	Pure lifestyle seeker	Loyal lifestyle entrepreneurship

Fig. 7.1. Typology of Lifestyle Entrepreneurs.

individual or family business rather than a collective. Studies have shown how sports, events and festivals could create a niche market (Carson et al., 2018) and disrupt existing industry (Guercinia and Cova, 2018). The Finnmark Race in Norway, for example, not only promotes a dog sledding event but also revitalises the tourism industry in the country more widely (Jæger, 2020). Similarly, the annual surf festival in Ireland contributes positively to the local economy and regional development (Marchant and Mottiar, 2011). GoPro is another exemplar of how a community of enthusiasts inspire and support the birth of a revolutionary product that in this case disrupts the camera sector (Guercinia and Cova, 2018). Like loyal lifestyle entrepreneurs, tribal lifestyle entrepreneurship caters to a niche market; the main difference is that tribal entrepreneurship is open to the idea of business expansion and actively engages with a community of like-minded enthusiasts. Future research is also needed to examine commonalities and differences in tribal lifestyle entrepreneurship between developing and industrialised countries.

Another note about categorising entrepreneurs is that opportunist and pure lifestyle seekers represent groups of lifestyle entrepreneurs who have little or no interest in the business they have created. They enter the market for a variety of reasons, namely autonomy, low entry barriers and low perceived risk. The main difference between opportunist and purist is in the opportunist's growth-mindedness and readiness to scale up their businesses.

Naturally, entrepreneurs' motivation, passion and their orientation towards growth have many overlapping dimensions. These are summarised in Fig. 7.2 that shows lifestyle entrepreneurs could be categorised based on their attitudes and behaviours.

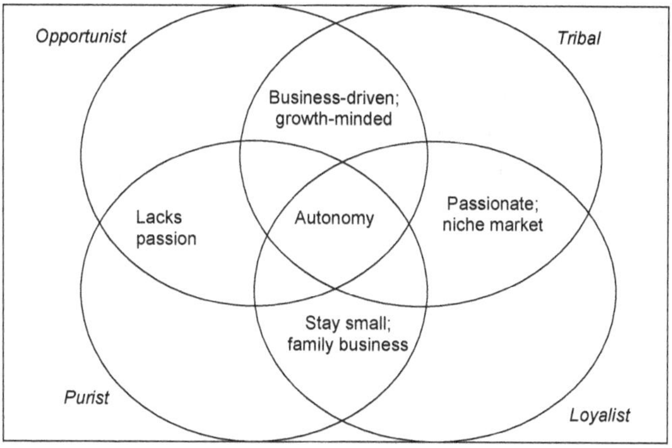

Fig. 7.2. An Emergent Classification of Lifestyle Entrepreneurs.

CONCLUSION: CAN LIFESTYLE ENTREPRENEURS CONTRIBUTE TO A REVITALISATION OF DEPRIVED COMMUNITIES?

Lifestyle entrepreneurship could be approached from a range of different perspectives influenced by varying economic concepts. In many industrialised economies, entrepreneurship has been and is highly supported by policymakers and perceived positively by society. In contrast, in socialist economies entrepreneurial activities have been restricted legislatively and therefore perceived negatively by the general public (Skokic and Morrison, 2011). Although perceptions of entrepreneurship are slowly changing in transitional economies, the concept of lifestyle entrepreneurship is relatively new to them (Skokic and Morrison, 2011; Xu and Feng, 2015; Sun and Xu, 2017). Some entrepreneurs even reject the idea of creating a new venture driven by personal and lifestyle considerations, i.e. by factors other than objective economics (Skokic and Morrison, 2011). Defining lifestyle entrepreneurship in a typical way, as being based on the entrepreneur's motivation and intention not to pursue growth, is therefore problematic because it overlooks the cultural context.

Cultural and economic peculiarities lead to different entrepreneurial attitudes towards quality of life and desired lifestyle. For some entrepreneurs, the preferred lifestyle is associated with counter-urban living (Carson et al., 2018), while for others it relates to the desire for frequent travel (Marchant and Mottiar, 2011) or for spending time with family (Lashley and Rowson, 2010). In industrialised countries, such as Italy and the United Kingdom, it is common to involve family members in lifestyle entrepreneurship (Shaw and Williams, 2004; Lashley and Rowson, 2010; Dominici et al., 2019). The reasons for family involvement are diverse but not seen as problematic, whereas entrepreneurs in transitioning economies, e.g. Croatia, would avoid family involvement and instead would give preference to hiring qualified outsiders (Skokic and Morrison, 2011). The emergent categorisation of lifestyle entrepreneurs attempts to look beyond the classical behavioural preferences and pay attention to entrepreneurial passion and volume of offerings (of service or products).

It is also worth emphasising that lifestyle entrepreneurs are not a homogeneous group, especially in the recently formed context of the digital economy, but a heterogeneous cohort of individuals who prioritise lifestyle over any other characteristics of entrepreneurial process.

After consolidation of all identified characteristics of lifestyle entrepreneurship into a model of enterprise culture in deprived communities the following structure emerges. The factors stimulating entrepreneurial activities in deprived communities are centred on the needs of the neighbourhood as it represents the primary target market. Lifestyle entrepreneurs tend to employ fewer people, but these employees are often recruited in/from the same area, which has a positive impact on local employment and relationships with the area, particularly in deprived locations.

The key factors hindering enterprising in deprived areas are lack of aspiration to growth and disregard of local market opportunities. Lack of growth orientation may affect negatively the availability of local products or services in deprived areas and may result in disregarding changing social needs in a locality. Furthermore, being an integral part of a local community, lifestyle entrepreneurs are aware of market opportunities but may lack an intent to pursue them.

This suggests that, although lifestyle entrepreneurs may integrate well into a deprived community, they would not necessarily abandon their lifestyle orientation for the sake of community values or needs. As it is unlikely that lifestyle entrepreneurs would aim for growth of their ventures, local and regional agencies in charge of economic development might focus on identification of opportunities for launching micro-enterprises and contribution to neighbourhoods' welfare, which would be aligned with motivation and desired volume of effort this category of entrepreneurs is prepared to put in. In deprived communities, effective promotion of these opportunities and the niche-oriented business models to lifestyle entrepreneurs is key.

LEARNING POINTS

- Since lifestyle entrepreneurs prioritise quality of life and social value, providing them with opportunities to contribute to value creation for a local community and reduce deprivation is likely to be in sync with their own values, which might support their business ideas and benefit the communities at the same time.
- As lifestyle reflects personal attitudes towards people and the environment, promoting opportunities to make a change in a deprived community might appeal to lifestyle

entrepreneurs and trigger the launch of a small venture. Emphasising recognition that would stem from improving lives of disadvantaged populations and/or from changing conditions in the locality to the better might serve as a powerful tool for mobilising lifestyle entrepreneurs.

- Lifestyle entrepreneurs' initial reluctance to grow their businesses could eventually transform into intent to grow, for the benefit of disadvantaged populations and localities, should personal motivation and conditions change. Local governing bodies might significantly increase lifestyle entrepreneurs' contribution to revitalisation of deprived communities by influencing these conditions and motivation.

REFERENCES

Anderson, A. and McAuley, A. 1999. Marketing landscapes: the social context, *Qualitative Market Research: An International Journal*, 2(3), 176–188.

Ateljevic, I. and Doorne, S. 2000. Staying within the fence: lifestyle entrepreneurship in tourism, *Journal of Sustainable Tourism*, 8(5), 378–392.

Attree, K.J., McMullen, C. and Kleinschafer, J.L. 2018. Case study: Beavo's Honey – to grow, or not to grow, that is the question, *Small Enterprise Research*, 25(3), 303–307.

Bolton, B. and Thompson, J. 2003. *The Entrepreneurs in Focus: Achieve Your Potential*, London, UK, Thomson Learning.

Botsman, R. and Rogers, R. 2010. Beyond zipcar: collaborative consumption, *Harvard Business Review*, 88(10), 30.

Bredvold, R. and Skålén, P. 2016. Lifestyle entrepreneurs and their identity construction: a study of the tourism industry, *Tourism Management*, 56, 96–105.

Brush, C.G. and Chaganti, R. 1996. Cooperative strategies in non-high-tech new ventures: an exploratory study, *Entrepreneurship: Theory and Practice*, 21(2), 37–54.

Burns, P. 2001. *Entrepreneurship and Small Business*, Basingstoke, Palgrave Macmillan.

Carson, D.A., Carson, D.B. and Eimermann, M. 2018. International winter tourism entrepreneurs in northern Sweden: understanding migration, lifestyle, and business motivations, *Scandinavian Journal of Hospitality and Tourism*, 18(2), 183–198.

Casson, M. 2003. *The Entrepreneur: An Economic Theory*, 2nd ed., Cheltenham, Edward Elgar.

Cederholm, E.A. and Hultman, J. 2010. The value of intimacy – negotiating commercial relationships in lifestyle entrepreneurship, *Scandinavian Journal of Hospitality and Tourism*, 10(1), 16–32.

Claire, L. 2012. Re-storying the entrepreneurial ideal: lifestyle entrepreneurs as hero? *Tamara: Journal for Critical Organization Inquiry*, 10(1–2), 31–39.

Dahles, H. and Bras, K. 1999. Entrepreneurs in romance: tourism in Indonesia, *Annals of Tourism Research*, 26(2), 267–293.

Dewhurst, P. and Horobin, H. 1998. Small business owners. In *The Management of Small Tourism and Hospitality Firms*, Ed. R. Thomas, pp. 19–38, London, Cassell.

Dominici, A., Boncinelli, F. and Marone, E. 2019. Lifestyle entrepreneurs in winemaking, *International Journal of Wine Business Research*, 31(3), 385–405.

Fletcher, M. and Harris, S. 2002. Seven aspects of strategy formation: exploring the value of planning, *International Small Business Journal*, 20(3), 297–314

Glancey, K. 1998. Determinants of growth and profitability in small entrepreneurial firms, *International Journal of Entrepreneurial Behaviour & Research*, 4(1), 18–27.

Gray, C. 2006. Absorptive capacity, knowledge management and innovation in entrepreneurial small firms, *International Journal of Entrepreneurial Behaviour & Research*, 12(6), 345–360.

Greenbank, P. 2001. Objective setting in the micro-business, *International Journal of Entrepreneurial Behaviour & Research*, 7(3), 108–127.

Guercinia, S. and Cova, B. 2018. Unconventional entrepreneurship, *Journal of Business Research*, 92, 385–391.

Hyatt, J. and Mamis, R. 1997. Profile of Bootstrappers, Inc., *Magazine*, 61–63.

Jæger, K. 2020. Event start-ups as catalysts for place, sport and tourism development: moment scapes and geographical considerations, *Sport in Society*, 23(1), 40–55. doi: 10.1080/17430437.2018.1555218

Kuratko, D.F. 2008. *Entrepreneurship: Theory, Process, and Practice*, 8th ed., Mason, OH, Cengage Learning.

Lashley, C. and Rowson, B. 2010. Lifestyle businesses: insights into Blackpool's hotel sector, *International Journal of Hospitality Management*, 29(3), 511–519.

Lerner, M. and Almor, T. 2002. Relationships among strategic capabilities and the performance of women-owned small ventures, *Journal of Small Business Management*, 40(2), 109–125.

Locke, E.A. and Latham, G.P. 2006. New directions in goal-setting theory, *Current Directions in Psychological Science*, 15(5), 265–268.

Low, M.B. and MacMillian, I.C. 1988. Entrepreneurship: past research and future challenge, *Journal of Management*, 14(2), 139–161.

Macrì, D.M., Tagliaventi, M.R. and Bertolotti, F. 2002. A grounded theory for resistance to change in a small organization, *Journal of Organizational Change Management*, 15(3), 292–310.

Marchant, B. and Mottiar, Z. 2011. Understanding lifestyle entrepreneurs and digging beneath the issue of profits: profiling surf tourism lifestyle entrepreneurs in Ireland, *Tourism Planning & Development*, 8(2), 171–183.

Maslow, A. 1943. A theory of human motivation, *Psychological Review*, 50(4), 370–396.

McClelland, D.C. 1987. *Human Motivation*, Cambridge, Cambridge University Press.

McGinn, D. 2005. The trouble with lifestyle entrepreneurs, *Inc.*, 27(7), 21–23.

Milanesi, M. 2018. Exploring passion in hobby-related entrepreneurship. Evidence from Italian cases, *Journal of Business Research*, 92, 423–430.

Mottiar, Z. 2007. Lifestyle entrepreneurs and spheres of inter-firm relations: the case of Westport, Co Mayo, Ireland, *The International Journal of Entrepreneurship and Innovation*, 8(1), 67–74.

Rogers, S. and Makonnen, R. 2002. *The Entrepreneur's Guide to Finance and Business: Wealth Creation Techniques for Growing a Business*, Highstown, NJ, McGraw-Hill Professional.

Segal, G., Borgia, D. and Schoenfeld, J. 2005. The motivation to become an entrepreneur, *International Journal of Entrepreneurial Behaviour & Research*, 11(1), 42–57.

Shaw, G. and Williams, A.M. 2004. From lifestyle consumption to lifestyle production: changing patterns of tourism entrepreneurship. In *Advances in Tourism Research: Small Firms in Tourism*, Ed. R. Thomas, pp. 99–113, Amsterdam, Elsevier.

Skokic, V. and Morrison, A. 2011. Conceptions of tourism lifestyle entrepreneurship: transition economy context, *Tourism Planning & Development*, 8(2), 157–169.

Smallbone, D., Leig, R. and North, D. 1995. The characteristics and strategies of high growth SMEs, *International Journal of Entrepreneurial Behaviour & Research*, 1(3), 44–62.

Smith, N.R. and Miner, J.B. 1983. Type of entrepreneur, type of firm, and managerial motivation: implications for organizational life cycle theory, *Strategic Management Journal*, 4(4), 325–340.

Sun, X. and Xu, H. 2017. Lifestyle tourism entrepreneurs' mobility motivations: a case study on Dali and Lijiang, China, *Tourism Management Perspectives*, 24, 64–71.

Swedberg, R. 2000. *Entrepreneurship: The Social Science View*, Oxford, Oxford University Press.

Vroom, V.H. 2005. On the origins of expectancy theory. In *Great Minds in Management: The Process of Theory Development*, Eds K.G. Smith and M.A. Hitt, pp. 239–260, Oxford, Oxford University Press.

Xu, H. and Feng, Q. 2015. The production and consumption of home meals in the home restaurants in Guangzhou, *Journal of China Tourism Research*, 11(1), 105–120.

Yang, K. 2007. *Entrepreneurship in China*. Hampshire, Ashgate Publishing, Ltd.

8

CONCLUSION: INTEGRATIVE APPROACH TO ENTERPRISE DEVELOPMENT IN DEPRIVED COMMUNITIES – LESSONS LEARNED

This concluding chapter looks at the big picture: it delineates principal learning outcomes stemming from the book's discussion of how to foster entrepreneurship in deprived communities; identifies critical questions in enterprise development requiring innovative approaches and further debate; and discusses broader considerations and future research opportunities. Summarising the book's core argument, this chapter highlights a guiding framework for revitalising deprived areas and assisting disadvantaged populations. Although the framework might be used across the nations, networks and contexts, the exact methods and tools for the design of stimulating programmes and their implementation might vary, leaving room for local initiative, flexibility and innovation (Brown et al., 2001; Dubina and Carayannis, 2016; Bliemel et al., 2019).

LESSONS FOR ENTERPRISE DEVELOPMENT

- *As there is no single most effective recipe for fostering enterprise in deprived communities, an integrative approach embracing a range of methods and tools offers more opportunities to the neighbourhoods and all those who might be appealed and motivated by these methods.*

Each community or disadvantaged group has its special traits and it is often impossible to argue upfront that a certain arrangement or stimulus will produce the desired outcome, for example, a number of start-ups in a particular sector or area. Some tools that proved effective for a specific community may have little or no impact for a similar kind of community in another context or a different country. Furthermore, in the same community methods that earlier worked well may lose their impact after some time as conditions, regulations and mindset change. Therefore, integrating a broad collection of methods into a comprehensive set that would be tailored to the needs of a community and reflect its specifics should be viewed as a preferred approach to developing entrepreneurship (Fernández-Serrano et al., 2018; O'Connor et al., 2018).

- *Integrative approach to enterprise development should not transform in the mere gathering of all kinds of tools that might trigger small venture creation by various groups, e.g. seniors or lifestyle entrepreneurs. In integrative approach, the core is entrepreneurial culture that, once embedded in the community, should serve as a fertile ground encouraging people to engage in creative business practice.*

As a set of habits, traditions, typical behaviours, norms and values, all leading to entrepreneurial activity, entrepreneurial culture is critical for the formation of the context that would permit to embark on a journey from deprivation to prosperity (Berger, 1991; Beugelsdijk, 2007; Blideanu and Diaconescu, 2018). While embracing many methods, programmes and incentives for aspiring entrepreneurs, an integrative approach needs to steer various tools to ensure embeddedness of entrepreneurial culture. It is crucial because prevailing culture will, in turn, ensure continuity of entrepreneurship (Roundy et al., 2017). Without continuity, after certain, perhaps quite effective, enterprise support programmes end, incentives may not appear powerful enough, and efforts to foster new firm creation might have ended up with no tangible results (Hayton and Cacciotti, 2013). If so, deprived communities might return to their earlier conditions, with little or no entrepreneurship. As such, support programmes are unable to ensure sustainable entrepreneurship as they normally focus on kick-starting enterprise in certain sectors and/or by certain groups, for example, young people or unemployed women. Sustainability of creative business practices, with ongoing new venture creation, stems from entrepreneurial culture that is central for the entrepreneurial ecosystem (Auerswald, 2015; Acs et al., 2017; Alvedalen and Boschma, 2017; Audretsch and Belitski, 2017; Audretsch et al., 2018; Çalıyurt and Segura, 2020). Although the discussion of entrepreneurial ecosystem, its elements and traits is beyond this book's scope, each chapter emphasised factors that may facilitate entrepreneurship in deprived communities. Undoubtedly, these factors are part of the broader framework that is typically viewed as an ecosystem for entrepreneurship.

- *Integrative approach requires engaging all actors who might be instrumental for developing entrepreneurship, with the understanding that their roles might be evolving during the joint effort in a deprived community.*

In addition to local governments and regional agencies, these actors might include, for example, schools, local activists and social entrepreneurs. This book highlighted a case in Ukraine where a joint programme, aimed at development of youth entrepreneurship in the rural area, was successfully implemented by collaborative work of the local government, social entrepreneurs and local schools, delivering training in launching and running a business to school pupils. Mobilising various actors requires more than just a common goal, i.e. to improve conditions in a deprived community. It requires creating motivation for various actors and linking these motivations to produce synergistic effect. This way the outcomes for deprived communities might be maximised.

- *Drawing on the lesson about ensuring synergistic effect, it is worth emphasising the importance of networks and networking in deprived communities.*

Each actor might have limited capacity to organise, finance and promote a project fostering enterprise in a deprived community. In contrast, networks permit to join forces, better identify opportunities for new ventures in a broad spectrum of themes and implement projects focusing on factors facilitating entrepreneurship (Minguzzi and Passaro, 2001; Feld, 2012). Networks are useful for sharing resources but also for drawing on each actor's expertise and creativity. Particularly instrumental for identifying opportunities that could be channelled to aspiring entrepreneurs and all those who are interested in revitalising deprived communities, networks are also critically important for developing and enabling entrepreneurial culture (Breazeale et al., 2015; Dimitratos et al., 2016; Capelleras et al., 2019).

- *Local governing bodies need to pay special attention to encouraging innovation, particularly in motivating and supporting those who are entertaining entrepreneurial ideas* (Schwarzkopf, 2016; Fritsch and Wyrwich, 2018).

One method to accomplish this is by partnering with social entrepreneurs and NGOs and co-sponsoring their grant-making activity. The latter is typically a powerful tool to foster engagement of many population groups in revitalisation of the locality and assisting disadvantaged people. To provide incentives to entrepreneurial endeavours and steer efforts in a certain direction, local governments can use their non-cash resources (e.g. abandoned buildings, unused land) and provide administrative support. Mobilising social entrepreneurship and drawing on active citizenship in many cases have proven to be an effective tool for making improvements in deprived communities.

FUTURE RESEARCH

Although this book has provided insights into a range of aspects related to development of entrepreneurship in deprived communities, a significant volume of research and practical work has to be done to identify the effective approaches and best practice (Cavallo et al., 2018). It is likely that different contexts may require different approaches, instruments and methods. Some salient questions requiring further research are: What are the contextual features of ecosystem that could be developed for a deprived community? What is the impact of local and national culture on enabling entrepreneurship in disadvantages areas? What are the critical success factors in mobilising and connecting different actors for community revitalisation? And, what are non-traditional, innovative methods of motivating people in various categories – rural, senior, necessity and lifestyle entrepreneurs? An interesting and useful area is international dimension of entrepreneurship and, more generally, best practice in revitalisation of deprived communities and assisting disadvantaged populations. What could be drawn from the experience of other localities and nations? Although some literature is available (e.g. Chaşovschi et al., 2014; Gabrielsson et al., 2014), academics and practitioners will benefit from more contributions.

Yet another opportunity not to be missed in research is in the field of digital entrepreneurship (Sussan and Acs, 2017). What is its role in revitalising deprived communities? How to provide effective support to those thinking about digital business? Can digital services provide tangible contribution to job creation in deprived areas? Future research and case studies in a range of contexts may provide answers to these and many other questions about the role of digital entrepreneurship. In a search for better tools for activating entrepreneurship in deprived communities, engaging people in productive activity with the use of digital technology, leading to income generation, might serve as one of the promising approaches that could deliver the desired outcomes.

REFERENCES

Acs, Z., Stam, E., Audretsch, D. and O'Connor, A. 2017. The lineages of the entrepreneurial ecosystem approach, *Small Business Economics*, 49(1), 1–10.

Alvedalen, J. and Boschma, R. 2017. A critical review of entrepreneurial ecosystems research: towards a future research agenda, *European Planning Studies*, 25(6), 887–903.

Audretsch, D. and Belitski, B. 2017. Entrepreneurial ecosystems in cities: establishing the framework conditions, *The Journal of Technology Transfer*, 42(5), 1030–1051.

Audretsch, D., Mason, C., Miles, M. and O'Connor, A. 2018. The dynamics of entrepreneurial ecosystems, *Entrepreneurship & Regional Development*, 30(3–4), 471–474.

Auerswald, P. 2015. Enabling entrepreneurial ecosystems. In *The Oxford Handbook of Local Competitiveness*, Eds D. Audretsch, A. Link and M.L. Walsok, pp. 54–83, Oxford, Oxford University Press.

Berger, B. Ed. 1991. *The Culture of Entrepreneurship*, San Francisco, CA, ICS Press.

Beugelsdijk, S. 2007. Entrepreneurial culture, regional innovativeness and economic growth, *Journal of Evolutionary Economics*, 17(2), 187–210.

Blideanu, D. and Diaconescu, M. 2018. The entrepreneurial culture in Europe – new challenges in the new economy, *The Romanian Economic Journal*, XXI(68), 2–18.

Bliemel, M., Flores, R., De Klerk, S. and Miles, M.P. 2019. Accelerators as start-up infrastructure for entrepreneurial clusters, *Entrepreneurship & Regional Development*, 31(1–2), 133–149.

Breazeale, N., Fortunato, M.W.-P., Allen, J.E., Hustedde, R.J. and Pushkarskaya, H. 2015. Constructing a multidimensional measure of local entrepreneurial culture, *Community Development*, 46(5), 516–540.

Brown, T.E., Davidsson, P. and Wiklund, J. 2001. An operationalization of Stevenson's conceptualization of entrepreneurship as opportunity-based firm behavior, *Strategic Management Journal*, 22(10), 953–968.

Çalıyurt, K. and Segura, L. Eds 2020. *Women, Sustainable Entrepreneurship and the Economy: A Global Perspective*, Abingdon, Routledge.

Capelleras, J.-L., Contin-Pilart, I., Larraza-Kintana, M. and Martin-Sanchez, V. 2019. Entrepreneurs' human capital and growth aspirations: the moderating role of regional entrepreneurial culture, *Small Business Economics*, 52(1), 3–25.

Cavallo, A., Ghezzi, A. and Balocco, R. 2018. Entrepreneurial ecosystem research: present debates and future directions, *The International Entrepreneurship and Management Journal*, 3(2), 1–31.

Chaşovschi, C., Bordeianu, O. and Clipa, D. 2014. Entrepreneurial culture in transition economies. The case of Romania and Republic of Moldova, *Procedia Economics and Finance*, 15, 1507–1514.

Dimitratos, P., Johnson, J.E., Plakoyiannaki, E. and Young, S. 2016. SME internationalization: how does the opportunity-based international entrepreneurial culture matter? *International Business Review*, 25(6), 1211–1222.

Dubina, I.N. and Carayannis, E.G. Eds 2016. *Creativity, Innovation, and Entrepreneurship Across Cultures: Theory and Practices*, New York, NY, Springer.

Feld, B. 2012. *Startup Communities: Building an Entrepreneurial Ecosystem in Your City*, New York, NY, John Wiley & Sons.

Fernández-Serrano, J., Berbegal, V., Velasco, F. and Expósito, A. 2018. Efficient entrepreneurial culture: a cross-country analysis of developed countries, *The International Entrepreneurship and Management Journal*, 14(1), 105–127.

Fritsch, M. and Wyrwich, M. 2018. Regional knowledge, entrepreneurial culture, and innovative start-ups over time and space–an empirical investigation, *Small Business Economics*, 51(2), 337–353.

Gabrielsson, M., Gabrielsson, P. and Dimitratos, P. 2014. International entrepreneurial culture and growth of international new ventures, *Management International Review*, 54(4), 445–471.

Hayton, J.C. and Cacciotti, G. 2013. Is there an entrepreneurial culture? A review of empirical research, *Entrepreneurship & Regional Development*, 25(9–10), 708–731.

Minguzzi, A. and Passaro, R. 2001. The network of relationships between the economic environment and the entrepreneurial culture in small firms, *Journal of Business Venturing*, 16(2), 181–207.

O'Connor, A., Stam, E., Sussan, F. and Audretsch, D.B. Eds 2018. *Entrepreneurial Ecosystems: Place-Based Transformations and Transitions*, Cham, Springer.

Roundy, P.T., Brockman, B.K. and Bradshaw, M. 2017. The resilience of entrepreneurial ecosystems, *Journal of Business Venturing Insights*, 8, 99–104.

Schwarzkopf, C. 2016. *Fostering Innovation and Entrepreneurship: Entrepreneurial Ecosystem and Entrepreneurial Fundamentals in the USA and Germany*, Wiesbaden, Springer.

Sussan, F. and Acs, Z. 2017. The digital entrepreneurial ecosystem, *Small Business Economics*, 49(1), 55–73.

INDEX

www.ingramcontent.com/pod-product-compliance
Lightning Source LLC
La Vergne TN
LVHW022210200926
848481LV00006B/1914
* 9 7 8 1 7 8 9 7 3 9 8 8 6 *